John

A LIFE APPLICATION ® BIBLE STUDY

Part 1:
Complete text of John with study notes
from the *Life Application Bible*

Part 2:
Thirteen lessons for individual or group study

Study questions written and edited by
REV. ED TRENNER
DR. JAMES C. GALVIN
REV. DAVID R. VEERMAN
DR. BRUCE B. BARTON

Tyndale House Publishers, Inc.
Wheaton, Illinois

Life Application Bible Studies

Genesis TLB	**Matthew** NIV	**Philippians & Colossians** NIV
Joshua TLB	**Mark** TLB & NIV	**1 & 2 Thessalonians &**
Judges NIV	**Luke** NIV	**Philemon** NIV
Ruth & Esther TLB	**John** NIV	**1 & 2 Timothy & Titus** NIV
1 Samuel NIV	**Acts** TLB & NIV	**Hebrews** NIV
Ezra & Nehemiah NIV	**Romans** NIV	**James** NIV
Proverbs NIV	**1 Corinthians** NIV	**1 & 2 Peter & Jude** NIV
Daniel NIV	**2 Corinthians** NIV	**1 & 2 & 3 John** NIV
Hosea & Jonah TLB	**Galatians & Ephesians** NIV	**Revelation** NIV

Front cover photo by Christopher Talbot Frank

ISBN 0-8423-2717-7

Printed in the United States of America

97 96 95
16 15 14 13 12 11 10 9

NOTES

In addition to providing the reader with many application notes, the *Life Application Bible* offers several explanatory notes that help the reader understand culture, history, context, difficult-to-understand passages, background, places, theological concepts, and the relationship of various passages in Scripture to other passages.

BOOK INTRODUCTION

The Book Introduction is divided into several easy-to-find parts:

Timeline. A guide that puts the Bible book into its historical setting. It lists the key events and the dates when they occurred.

Vital Statistics. A list of straight facts about the book—those pieces of information you need to know at a glance.

Overview. A summary of the book with general lessons and applications that can be learned from the book as a whole.

Blueprint. The outline of the book. It is printed in easy-to-understand language and is designed for easy memorization. To the right of each main heading is a key lesson that is taught in that particular section.

Megathemes. A section that gives the main themes of the Bible book, explains their significance, and then tells why they are still important for us today.

Map. If included, this shows the key places found in that book and retells the story of the book from a geographical perspective.

OUTLINE

The *Life Application Bible* has a new, custom-made outline that was designed specifically from an application point of view. Several unique features should be noted:

1. To avoid confusion and to aid memory work, the book outline has only three levels for headings. Main outline heads are marked with a capital letter. Subheads are marked by a number. Minor explanatory heads have no letter or number.

2. Each main outline head marked by a letter also has a brief paragraph below it summarizing the Bible text and offering a general application.

3. Parallel passages are listed where they apply.

PERSONALITY PROFILES
Another unique feature of this Bible is the profiles of key Bible people, including their strengths and weaknesses, greatest accomplishments and mistakes, and key lessons from their lives.

MAPS
The *Life Application Bible* has a thorough and comprehensive Bible atlas built right into the book. There are two kinds of maps: A book introduction map, telling the story of the book, and thumbnail maps in the notes, plotting most geographic movements.

CHARTS AND DIAGRAMS
Many charts and diagrams are included to help the reader better visualize difficult concepts or relationships. Most charts not only present the needed information but show the significance of the information as well.

CROSS-REFERENCES
A carefully organized cross-reference system in the margins of the Bible text helps the reader find related passages quickly.

TEXTUAL NOTES
Directly related to the text of the New International Version, the textual notes provide explanations on certain wording in the translation, alternate translations, and information about readings in the ancient manuscripts.

HIGHLIGHTED NOTES
In each Bible study lesson you will be asked to read specific notes as part of your preparation. These notes have been highlighted by a bullet (•) so that you can find them easily.

This book of John is part of the *New International Version* of the Holy Bible, a completely new translation made by over a hundred scholars working directly from the best available Greek texts. It had its beginning in 1965 when, after several years of exploratory study by committees from the Christian Reformed Church and the National Association of Evangelicals, a group of scholars met at Palos Heights, Illinois, and concurred in the need for a new translation of the Bible in contemporary English. This group, though not made up of official church representatives, was transdenominational. Its conclusion was endorsed by a large number of leaders from many denominations who met in Chicago in 1966.

Responsibility for the new version was delegated by the Palos Heights group to a self-governing body of fifteen, the Committee on Bible Translation, composed for the most part of biblical scholars from colleges, universities and seminaries. In 1967 the New York Bible Society (now the International Bible Society) generously undertook the financial sponsorship of the project—a sponsorship that made it possible to enlist the help of many distinguished scholars. The fact that participants from the United States, Great Britain, Canada, Australia and New Zealand worked together gave the project its international scope. That they were from many denominations—including Anglican, Assemblies of God, Baptist, Brethren, Christian Reformed, Church of Christ, Evangelical Free, Lutheran, Mennonite, Methodist, Nazarene, Presbyterian, Wesleyan, and other churches—helped to safeguard the translation from sectarian bias.

How it was made helps to give the New International Version its distinctiveness. The translation of each book was assigned to a team of scholars. Next, one of the Intermediate Editorial Committees revised the initial translation, with constant reference to the Hebrew, Aramaic, or Greek. Their work then went to one of the General Editorial Committees, which checked it in detail and made another thorough revision. This revision in turn was carefully reviewed by the Committee on Bible Translation, which made further changes and then released the final version for publication. In this way the entire Bible underwent three revisions, during each of which the translation was examined for its faithfulness to the original languages and for its English style.

All this involved many thousands of hours of research and discussion regarding the meaning of the texts and the precise way of putting them into English. It may well be that no other translation has been made by a more thorough process of review and revision from committee to committee than this one.

From the beginning of the project, the Committee on Bible Translation held to certain goals for the New International Version: that it would be an accurate translation and one that would have clarity and literary quality and so prove suitable for public and private reading, teaching, preaching, memorizing and liturgical use. The Committee also sought to preserve some measure of continuity with the long tradition of translating the Scriptures into English.

In working toward these goals, the translators were united in their commitment to the authority and infallibility of the Bible as God's Word in written form. They believe that it contains the divine answer to the deepest needs of humanity, that it sheds unique light on our path in a dark world, and that it sets forth the way to our eternal well-being.

The first concern of the translators has been the accuracy of the translation and its fidelity to the thought of the biblical writers. They have striven for more than a word-for-word translation. Because thought patterns and syntax differ from language to language, faithful communication of the meaning of the writers of the Bible

demands frequent modifications in sentence structure and constant regard for the contextual meanings of words.

The Committee on Bible Translation submitted the developing version to a number of stylistic consultants. Samples of the translation were tested for clarity and ease of reading by various kinds of people—young and old, highly educated and less well educated, ministers and laymen. Concern for clear and natural English motivated the translators and consultants. In view of the international use of English, the translators sought to avoid obvious Americanisms on the one hand and obvious Anglicisms on the other. A British edition reflects the comparatively few differences of significant idiom and of spelling.

As for the traditional pronouns "thou," "thee" and "thine" in reference to the Deity, the translators judged that to use these archaisms (along with the old verb forms such as "doest," "wouldest" and "hadst") would violate accuracy in translation. Greek does not use special pronouns for the persons of the Godhead. A present-day translation is not enhanced by forms that in the time of the King James Version were used in everyday speech, whether referring to God or man.

The Greek text used in translating the New Testament was an eclectic one. No other piece of ancient literature has such an abundance of manuscript witnesses as does the New Testament. Where existing manuscripts differ, the translators made their choice of readings according to accepted principles of New Testament textual criticism. Footnotes call attention to places where there was uncertainty about what the original text was. The best current printed texts of the Greek New Testament were used.

There is a sense in which the work of translation is never wholly finished. This applies to all great literature and uniquely so to the Bible. In 1973 the New Testament in the New International Version was published. Since then, suggestions for corrections and revisions have been received from various sources. The Committee on Bible Translation carefully considered the suggestions and adopted a number of them. These were incorporated in the first printing of the entire Bible in 1978. Additional revisions were made by the Committee on Bible Translation in 1983 and appear in printings after that date.

To achieve clarity the translators sometimes supplied words not in the original texts but required by the context. If there was uncertainty about such material, it is enclosed in brackets. Also for the sake of clarity or style, nouns, including some proper nouns, are sometimes substituted for pronouns, and vice versa. As an aid to the reader, italicized sectional headings are inserted in most of the books. They are not to be regarded as part of the NIV text, are not for oral reading, and are not intended to dictate the interpretation of the sections they head.

The footnotes in this version are of several kinds, most of which need no explanation. Those giving alternative translations begin with "Or" and generally introduce the alternative with the last word preceding it in the text, except when it is a single-word alternative; in poetry quoted in a footnote a slant mark indicates a line division. Footnotes introduced by "Or" do not have uniform significance. In some cases two possible translations were considered to have about equal validity. In other cases, though the translators were convinced that the translation in the text was correct, they judged that another interpretation was possible and of sufficient importance to be represented in a footnote. In the New Testament, footnotes that refer to uncertainty regarding the original text are introduced by "Some manuscripts" or similar expressions.

It should be noted that minerals, flora and fauna, architectural details, articles of clothing and jewelry, musical instruments and other articles cannot always be identified with precision. Also, measures of capacity in the biblical period are particularly uncertain.

Like all translations of the Bible, made as they are by imperfect man, this one

undoubtedly falls short of its goals. Yet we are grateful to God for the extent to which he has enabled us to realize these goals and for the strength he has given us and our colleagues to complete our task. We offer this version of the Bible to him in whose name and for whose glory it has been made. We pray that it will lead many into a better understanding of the Holy Scriptures and a fuller knowledge of Jesus Christ the incarnate Word, of whom the Scriptures so faithfully testify.

The Committee on Bible Translation

June 1978
(Revised August 1983)

Names of the translators and editors may be secured
from the International Bible Society,
translation sponsors of the New International Version,
P.O. Box 62970, Colorado Springs, Colorado, 80962-2970 U.S.A.

JOHN

JOHN

VITAL STATISTICS

PURPOSE:
To prove conclusively that Jesus is the Son of God and that all who believe in him will have eternal life

AUTHOR:
John, the apostle, son of Zebedee, brother of James, called a "Son of Thunder"

TO WHOM WRITTEN:
New Christians and searching non-Christians

DATE WRITTEN:
Probably A.D. 85–90

SETTING:
Written after the destruction of Jerusalem in A.D. 70 and before John's exile to the island of Patmos

KEY VERSES:
"Jesus did many other miraculous signs in the presence of his disciples, which are not recorded in this book. But these are written that you may believe that Jesus is the Christ, the Son of God, and that by believing you may have life in his name" (20:30, 31).

KEY PEOPLE:
Jesus, John the Baptist, the disciples, Mary, Martha, Lazarus, Jesus' mother, Pilate, Mary Magdalene

KEY PLACES:
Judean countryside, Samaria, Galilee, Bethany, Jerusalem

SPECIAL FEATURES:
Of the eight miracles recorded, six are unique (among the Gospels) to John, as is the "Upper Room Discourse" (chapters 14—17). Over 90% of John is unique to his Gospel— John does not contain a genealogy or any record of Jesus' birth, childhood, temptation, transfiguration, appointment of the disciples, and no parables, ascension, or Great Commission.

HE SPOKE and galaxies whirled into place, stars burned the heavens, and planets began orbiting their suns—words of awesome, unlimited, unleashed power. He spoke again and the waters and lands were filled with plants and creatures, running, swimming, growing, and multiplying— words of animating, breathing, pulsing life. Again he spoke and man and woman were formed, thinking, speaking, and loving—words of personal and creative glory. Eternal, infinite, unlimited—he was, is, and always will be the Maker and Lord of all that exists.

And then he came in the flesh to a speck in the universe called planet earth. The mighty Creator became a part of the creation, limited by time and space and susceptible to age, sickness, and death. But love propelled him, and so he came to rescue and save those who were lost and to give them the gift of eternity. He is *the Word;* he is Jesus, the Christ.

It is this truth that the apostle John brings to us in this book. John's Gospel is not a life of Christ; it is a powerful argument for the incarnation, a conclusive demonstration that Jesus was, and is, the very heaven-sent Son of God and the only source of eternal life.

John discloses Christ's identity with his very first words, "In the beginning was the Word, and the Word was with God, and the Word was God. He was with God in the beginning" (1:1, 2); and the rest of the book continues the theme. John, the eyewitness, chooses eight of Christ's miracles (or signs, as he calls them) to reveal Christ's divine/human nature and his life-giving mission. These signs are (1) turning water to wine (2:1–11), (2) healing the official's son (4:46–54), (3) healing the invalid at Bethesda (5:1–9), (4) feeding the 5,000 with just a few loaves and fish (6:1–14), (5) walking on the water (6:15–21), (6) restoring sight to the blind man (9:1–41), (7) raising Lazarus from the dead (11:1–44), and, after the resurrection, (8) giving the disciples an overwhelming catch of fish (21:1–14).

In every chapter Jesus' deity is revealed. And John underscores Jesus' true identity through the titles he is given—Word, the One and Only, Lamb of God, Son of God, true bread, life, resurrection, vine. And the formula is "I am." When Jesus uses this phrase, he affirms his preexistence and eternal deity. Jesus says, *I am* the bread of life (6:35); *I am* the light of the world (8:12; 9:5); *I am* the gate (10:7); *I am* the good shepherd (10:11, 14); *I am* the resurrection and the life (11:25); *I am* the way and the truth and the life (14:6); and *I am* the true vine (15:1).

The greatest sign, of course, is the resurrection, and John provides a stirring eyewitness account of finding the empty tomb. Then he records various post-resurrection appearances by Jesus.

John, the devoted follower of Christ, has given us a personal and powerful look at Jesus Christ, the eternal Son of God. As you read his story commit yourself to believe and follow him.

THE BLUEPRINT

A. BIRTH AND PREPARATION OF JESUS, THE SON OF GOD (1:1—2:11)

John makes it clear that Jesus is not just a man; he is the eternal Son of God. He is the light of the world because he offers this gift of eternal life to all mankind. How blind and foolish to call Jesus nothing more than an unusually good man or moral teacher. Yet we sometimes act as if this were true when we casually toss around his words and go about living our own way. If Jesus is the eternal Son of God, we should pay attention to his divine identity and life-giving message.

B. MESSAGE AND MINISTRY OF JESUS, THE SON OF GOD (2:12—12:50)
1. Jesus Encounters Belief and Unbelief From the People
2. Jesus Encounters Conflict With the Religious Leaders
3. Jesus Encounters Crucial Events in Jerusalem

Jesus meets with individuals, preaches to great crowds, trains his disciples, and debates with the religious leaders. The message, that he is the Son of God, receives a mixed reaction. Some worship him, some are puzzled, some shrink back, and some move to silence him. We see the same varied reactions today. Times have changed, but people's hearts remain hard. May we see ourselves in these encounters Jesus had with people, and may our response be to worship and follow him.

C. DEATH AND RESURRECTION OF JESUS, THE SON OF GOD (13:1—21:25)
1. Jesus Teaches His Disciples
2. Jesus Completes His Mission

Jesus carefully instructed the disciples how to continue to believe even after his death, yet they could not take it in. After he died and the first reports came back that Jesus was alive, the disciples could not believe it. Thomas is especially remembered as one who refused to believe even when he heard the eyewitness accounts from other disciples. May we not be like Thomas, demanding a physical face-to-face encounter, but may we accept the eyewitness of the disciples that John has recorded in this Gospel.

MEGATHEMES

THEME	EXPLANATION	IMPORTANCE
Jesus Christ, Son of God	John shows us that Jesus is unique as God's special Son, yet he is fully God. Because he is fully God, Jesus is able to reveal God to us clearly and accurately.	Because Jesus is God's Son, we can perfectly trust what he says. By trusting him, we can gain an open mind to understand God's message and fulfill his purpose in our lives.
Eternal life	Because Jesus is God, he lives forever. Before the world began, he lived with God, and he will reign forever with him. In John we see Jesus revealed in power and magnificence even before his resurrection.	Jesus offers eternal life to us. We are invited to begin living in a personal, eternal relationship with him that begins now. Although we must grow old and die, by trusting him we can have a new life that lasts forever.
Believe	John records eight specific signs or miracles that show the nature of Jesus' power and love. We see his power over everything created, and we see his love of all people. These signs encourage us to believe in him.	Believing is active, living, and continuous trust in Jesus as God. When we believe in his life, his words, his death, and his resurrection, we are cleansed from sin and receive power to follow him. But we must respond to him by believing.
Holy Spirit	Jesus taught his disciples that the Holy Spirit would come after he ascended from earth. The Holy Spirit would then indwell, guide, counsel, and comfort those who follow Jesus. Through the Holy Spirit, Christ's presence and power are multiplied in all who believe.	Through God's Holy Spirit we are drawn to him in faith. We must know the Holy Spirit to understand all Jesus taught. We can experience Jesus' love and guidance as we allow the Holy Spirit to do his work in us.

Resurrection   On the third day after he died, Jesus rose from the dead. This was verified by his disciples and many eyewitnesses. This reality changed the disciples from frightened deserters to dynamic leaders in the new church. This fact is the foundation of the Christian faith.

We can be changed as the disciples were and have confidence that our bodies will one day be raised to live with Christ forever. The same power that raised Christ to life can give us the ability to follow Christ each day.

KEY PLACES IN JOHN

John's story begins as John the Baptist ministers near Bethany (Bethabara) beyond the Jordan (1:28ff). Jesus also begins his ministry, talking to some of the men who would later become his 12 disciples. Jesus' ministry in Galilee began with a visit to a wedding in Cana (2:1ff). Then he went to Capernaum, which became his new home (2:12). He journeyed to Jerusalem for the special feasts (2:13) and there met with Nicodemus, a religious leader (3:1ff). When he left Judea, he traveled through Samaria and ministered to the Samaritans (4:1ff). Jesus did miracles in Galilee (4:46ff) and in Judea and Jerusalem (5:1ff). We follow him as he fed 5,000 near Bethsaida beside the Sea of Galilee (Sea of Tiberias) (6:1ff), walked on the water to his frightened disciples (6:16ff), preached through Galilee (7:1), returned to Jerusalem (7:2ff), preached beyond the Jordan in Perea (10:40), raised Lazarus from the dead in Bethany (11:1ff), and finally entered Jerusalem for the last time to celebrate the Passover with his disciples and give them key teachings about what was to come and how they should act. His last hours before his crucifixion were spent in the city (13:1ff), in the Garden of Gethsemane (18:1ff), and finally in various buildings in Jerusalem during his trial (18:12ff). He would be crucified, but he would rise again as he had promised.

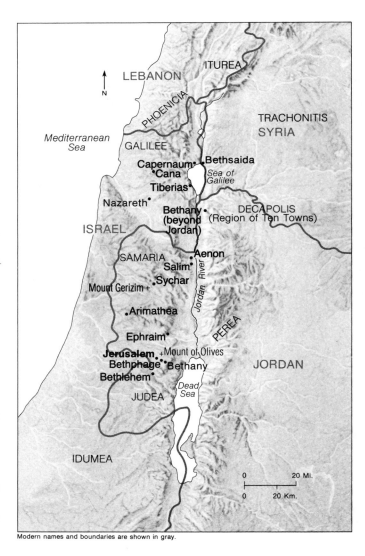

Modern names and boundaries are shown in gray.

A. BIRTH AND PREPARATION OF JESUS, THE SON OF GOD (1:1—2:11)

In this Gospel John provides clear evidence that Jesus is the Son of God and that by believing in him we may have eternal life. John also provides unique material about Jesus' birth. He did not come into being when he was born, because he is eternal.

The Word Became Flesh

1:1
Gen 1:1
Phil 2:6

1:3
1 Cor 8:6
Col 1:16,17
Heb 1:2

1:4
Jn 3:15,16,36
6:35,48; 8:12
11:25; 14:6

1:5
Jn 3:19; 9:5

1:7
Jn 5:33

1:9
1 Jn 2:8

1 In the beginning was the Word, and the Word was with God, and the Word was God. ²He was with God in the beginning.

³Through him all things were made; without him nothing was made that has been made. ⁴In him was life, and that life was the light of men. ⁵The light shines in the darkness, but the darkness has not understood*ᵃ* it.

⁶There came a man who was sent from God; his name was John. ⁷He came as a witness to testify concerning that light, so that through him all men might believe. ⁸He himself was not the light; he came only as a witness to the light. ⁹The true light that gives light to every man was coming into the world.*ᵇ*

¹⁰He was in the world, and though the world was made through him, the world did not recognize him. ¹¹He came to that which was his own, but his own did not receive him. ¹²Yet to all who received him, to those who believed in his name, he

ᵃ5 Or darkness, and the darkness has not overcome ᵇ9 Or This was the true light that gives light to every man who comes into the world

---

1:1ff What does John mean by *the Word? The Word* was a term used by theologians and philosophers, both Hebrew and Greek, in many different ways. In Hebrew Scripture, the Word was an agent of creation (Psalm 33:6), the source of God's message to his people through the prophets (Hosea 1:2), and God's law, his standard of holiness (Psalm 119:11). In Greek philosophy the Word was the divine essence that held all things together, God's ideal pattern for creation. John's description shows clearly that he is speaking of Jesus (see especially 1:14)—a human being he knew and loved, but at the same time the Creator of the universe, the ultimate revelation of God, the living picture of God's holiness, the one by whom "all things hold together" (Colossians 1:17). To Jewish readers, "the Word was God" was blasphemous. To Greek readers, "the Word became flesh" was unthinkable. To John, this new understanding of the Word was gospel, the Good News of Jesus Christ.

●**1:1** What Jesus taught and what he did are tied inseparably to who he is. John shows Jesus as fully human and fully God. Although Jesus took upon himself full humanity and lived as a man, he never ceased to be the eternal God who has always existed, the Creator and Sustainer of all things, and the source of eternal life. This is the truth about Jesus, and the foundation of all truth. If we cannot or do not believe this basic truth, we will not have enough faith to trust our eternal destiny to him. That is why John wrote this Gospel—to build faith and confidence in Jesus Christ so that we may believe he truly was and is the Son of God (20:30, 31).

1:1 John wrote to believers everywhere, both Jews and non-Jews (Gentiles). As one of Jesus' 12 disciples, John was an eyewitness, so his story is accurate. His book is not a biography (like the book of Luke) but a thematic presentation of Jesus' life. Many in John's original audience had a Greek background. Greek culture encouraged worship of many mythological gods, whose supernatural characteristics were as important to Greeks as genealogies were to Jews. John shows that Jesus is not only different from but superior to these gods of mythology.

1:3 When God created, he made something from nothing. Because we are created beings, we have no basis for pride. Remember that you exist only because God made you, and you have special gifts only because God gave them to you. With God you are something valuable and unique; apart from God you are nothing, because you are abandoning the purpose for which you were made.

●**1:3–5** Do you ever feel your life is too complex for God to understand? Remember, God created the entire universe, and nothing is too difficult for him. He created you, he is alive today, and his love

is bigger than any problem you may face.

●**1:4** Why is the life that was in Christ "the light of men"? Because death brings eternal darkness, and only Christ's eternal life planted in us will keep us alive in his new kingdom for eternity. Christ is eternally alive because he is God. He came to earth to offer mankind the hope and light of his eternal life. It can't be bought, only received as a gift. But Jesus gives it only to those who want it— those who want to live the way God's citizens will live in his future, eternal kingdom.

●**1:4, 5** "The darkness has not understood it" means the darkness of evil never has and never will overcome or extinguish God's light. Jesus Christ was the Creator of life, and his life brings light to mankind. In his light, we see ourselves as we really are (sinners in need of a Savior). When we follow Jesus, the light, we can avoid walking blindly and falling into sin. He lights the path ahead of us so we can see how to live. He removes the darkness of sin from our lives. Have you allowed the light of Christ to shine into your life? Let Christ guide your life, and you'll never need to stumble in darkness.

1:6–8 In this book, the name *John* refers to John the Baptist. For more information on John the Baptist, see his Profile in John 1.

●**1:8** We, like John the Baptist, are not the source of God's light; we merely reflect that light. Jesus Christ is the true light; he helps us see our way to God and shows us how to walk along that way. But Christ has chosen to reflect his light from his followers to an unbelieving world, perhaps because unbelievers are not able to bear the full blazing glory of his light firsthand. The word *witness* indicates our role as reflectors of Christ's light. We are never to present ourselves as the light to others, but are always to point them to Christ, the light.

1:10, 11 Although Christ created the world, the people he created didn't recognize him (1:10). Even the people chosen by God to prepare the rest of the world for the Messiah rejected him (1:11), although the entire Old Testament pointed to his coming.

1:12, 13 All who welcome Jesus Christ as Lord of their lives are reborn spiritually, receiving new life from God. Through faith in Christ, this new birth changes us from the inside out—rearranging our attitudes, desires, and motives. Being born makes you physically alive and places you in your parents' family (1:13). Being reborn makes you spiritually alive and puts you in God's family (1:12). Have you asked Christ to make you a new person? This fresh start in life is available to all who believe in Christ.

gave the right to become children of God— 13children born not of natural descent,*a* nor of human decision or a husband's will, but born of God.

14The Word became flesh and made his dwelling among us. We have seen his glory, the glory of the One and Only,*b* who came from the Father, full of grace and truth.

15John testifies concerning him. He cries out, saying, "This was he of whom I said, 'He who comes after me has surpassed me because he was before me.' " 16From the fullness of his grace we have all received one blessing after another. 17For the law was given through Moses; grace and truth came through Jesus Christ. 18No one has ever seen God, but God the One and Only,*b, c* who is at the Father's side, has made him known.

1:14
Ex 40:34,35
Rom 1:3; 8:3
Gal 4:4
Phil 2:6-8
Col 2:9
1 Tim 3:16
Heb 2:14
1 Jn 1:1; 4:2,3

1:18
Ex 33:20
2 Cor 4:4,6
Col 1:15

John the Baptist Denies Being the Christ

19Now this was John's testimony when the Jews of Jerusalem sent priests and Levites to ask him who he was. 20He did not fail to confess, but confessed freely, "I am not the Christ.*d*"

21They asked him, "Then who are you? Are you Elijah?"

He said, "I am not."

"Are you the Prophet?"

He answered, "No."

22Finally they said, "Who are you? Give us an answer to take back to those who sent us. What do you say about yourself?"

23John replied in the words of Isaiah the prophet, "I am the voice of one calling in the desert, 'Make straight the way for the Lord.' "*e*

24Now some Pharisees who had been sent 25questioned him, "Why then do you baptize if you are not the Christ, nor Elijah, nor the Prophet?"

1:20
Lk 3:15
Jn 3:28

1:21
Deut 18:15
Mal 4:5
Mt 11:14

1:23
Isa 40:3

a13 Greek *of bloods* *b14,18* Or *the Only Begotten* *c18* Some manuscripts *but the only* (or *only begotten*) *Son*
d20 Or *Messiah.* "The Christ" (Greek) and "the Messiah" (Hebrew) both mean "the Anointed One"; also in verse 25.
e23 Isaiah 40:3

●**1:14** "The Word became flesh" means becoming human. By doing so, Christ became (1) *the perfect teacher*—in Jesus' life we see how God thinks and therefore how we should think (Philippians 2:5–11); (2) *the perfect example*—as a model of what we are to become, he shows us how to live and gives us the power to live that way (1 Peter 2:21); (3) *the perfect sacrifice*—Jesus came as a sacrifice for all sins, and his death satisfied God's requirements for the removal of sin (Colossians 1:15–23).

●**1:14** "The One and Only [Son], who came from the Father" means Jesus is God's only and unique Son. The emphasis is on unique. Jesus is one of a kind and enjoys a relationship with God unlike all believers who are called "children" and said to be "born of God."

1:14 When Christ was born, God became a man. He was not part man and part God; he was completely human and completely divine (Colossians 2:9). Before Christ came, people could know God partially. After Christ came, people could know God fully because he became visible and tangible in Christ. Christ is the perfect expression of God in human form. The two most common errors people make about Jesus are to minimize his humanity or to minimize his divinity. Jesus is both God and man.

1:17 Law and grace are both aspects of God's nature that he uses in dealing with us. Moses emphasized God's law and justice, while Jesus Christ came to highlight God's mercy, love, and forgiveness. Moses could only be the giver of the law, while Christ came to fulfill it. The nature and will of God were revealed in the law; now the nature and will of God are revealed in Jesus Christ. Rather than coming through cold stone tablets, God's revelation ("truth") now comes through a person's life. As we get to know Christ better, our understanding of God will increase.

●**1:18** God communicated through various people in the Old Testament, usually prophets who were told to give specific messages. But no one ever *saw* God. In Christ, God revealed his nature and essence in a way that could be seen and touched. In Christ, God became a man who lived on earth.

1:19 The priests and Levites were respected religious leaders in Jerusalem. Priests served in the temple, and Levites assisted them. The leaders that came to see John were Pharisees (1:24), a group that both John the Baptist and Jesus often denounced. Many of them outwardly obeyed God's laws to look pious, while inwardly their hearts were filled with pride and greed. The Pharisees believed that their own oral traditions were just as important as God's inspired Word. For more information on the Pharisees, see the charts in Matthew 3 and Mark 2.

These leaders came to see John the Baptist for several reasons: (1) Their duty as guardians of the faith caused them to want to investigate any new preaching (Deuteronomy 13:1–5; 18:20–22). (2) They wanted to find out if he had the credentials of a prophet. (3) John had quite a following, and it was growing. They were probably jealous and wanted to see why this man was so popular.

1:21–23 In the Pharisees' minds, there were four options regarding John the Baptist's identity: he was (1) the prophet foretold by Moses (Deuteronomy 18:15), (2) Elijah (Malachi 4:5), (3) the Messiah, or (4) a false prophet. John denied being the first three personages. Instead he called himself, in the words of the Old Testament prophet Isaiah, "A voice of one calling: 'In the desert prepare the way for the Lord'" (Isaiah 40:3). The leaders kept pressing him to say who he was, because people were expecting the Messiah to come (Luke 3:15). But John emphasized only *why* he had come—to prepare the way for the Messiah. The Pharisees missed the point. They wanted to know who John was, but John wanted them to know who Jesus was.

1:25, 26 John was baptizing Jews. The Essenes (a strict, monastic sect of Judaism) practiced baptism for purification, but normally only non-Jews (Gentiles) were baptized when they converted to Judaism. When the Pharisees asked by what authority he was baptizing, they were asking who gave John the right to treat God's

1:26
Mt 3:11
Mk 1:8
Lk 3:16

1:28
Jn 3:26; 10:40

26"I baptize with*a* water," John replied, "but among you stands one you do not know. 27He is the one who comes after me, the thongs of whose sandals I am not worthy to untie."

28This all happened at Bethany on the other side of the Jordan, where John was baptizing.

a26 Or *in*; also in verses 31 and 33

JOHN THE BAPTIST

There's no getting around it—John the Baptist was unique. He wore odd clothes and ate strange food and preached an unusual message to the Judeans who went into the wastelands to see him.

But John did not aim at uniqueness for its own sake. Instead, he aimed at obedience. He knew he had a specific role to play in the world—announcing the coming of the Savior—and he put all his energies into this task. Luke tells us that John was in the desert when God's word of direction came to him. John was ready and waiting. The angel who had announced John's birth to Zechariah had made it clear this child was to be a Nazirite—one set apart for God's service. John remained faithful to that calling.

This wild-looking man had no power or position in the Jewish political system, but he spoke with almost irresistible authority. People were moved by his words because he spoke the truth, challenging them to turn from their sins and baptizing them as a symbol of their repentance. They responded by the hundreds. But even as people crowded to him, he pointed beyond himself, never forgetting that his main role was to announce the coming of the Savior.

The words of truth that moved many to repentance goaded others to resistance and resentment. John even challenged Herod to admit his sin. Herodias, the woman Herod had married illegally, decided to get rid of this desert preacher. Although she was able to have him killed, she was not able to stop his message. The One John had announced was already on the move. John had accomplished his mission.

God has given each of us a purpose for living, and we can trust him to guide us. John did not have the complete Bible as we know it today, but he focused his life on the truth he knew from the available Old Testament Scriptures. Likewise, we can discover in God's Word the truths he wants us to know. And as these truths work in us, others will be drawn to him. God can use you in a way he can use no one else. Let him know your willingness to follow him today.

Strengths and accomplishments:
• The God-appointed messenger to announce the arrival of Jesus
• A preacher whose theme was repentance
• A fearless confronter
• Known for his remarkable life-style
• Uncompromising

Lessons from his life:
• God does not guarantee an easy or safe life to those who serve him
• Doing what God desires is the greatest possible life investment
• Standing for the truth is more important than life itself

Vital statistics:
• Where: Judea
• Occupation: Prophet
• Relatives: Father: Zechariah. Mother: Elizabeth. Distant cousin: Jesus
• Contemporaries: Herod, Herodias

Key verse:
"I tell you the truth: Among those born of women there has not risen anyone greater than John the Baptist; yet he who is least in the kingdom of heaven is greater than he" (Matthew 11:11).

John's story is told in all four Gospels. His coming was predicted in Isaiah 40:3 and Malachi 4:5; and he is mentioned in Acts 1:5, 22; 10:37; 11:16; 13:24, 25; 18:25; 19:3, 4.

chosen people like Gentiles. John said, "I baptize with water"—he was merely helping the people perform a symbolic act of repentance. But soon one would come who would truly *forgive* sins, something only the Son of God—the Messiah—could do.

1:27 John the Baptist said he was not even worthy to be Christ's slave, to perform the humble task of unfastening his shoes. But in Luke 7:28, Jesus said that John was the greatest of all prophets. If such a great person felt inadequate even to be Christ's slave, how much more should we lay aside our pride to serve Christ! When we understand who Christ is, our pride and self-importance melt away.

Jesus the Lamb of God

29The next day John saw Jesus coming toward him and said, "Look, the Lamb of God, who takes away the sin of the world! 30This is the one I meant when I said, 'A man who comes after me has surpassed me because he was before me.' 31I myself did not know him, but the reason I came baptizing with water was that he might be revealed to Israel."

32Then John gave this testimony: "I saw the Spirit come down from heaven as a dove and remain on him. 33I would not have known him, except that the one who sent me to baptize with water told me, 'The man on whom you see the Spirit come down and remain is he who will baptize with the Holy Spirit.' 34I have seen and I testify that this is the Son of God."

1:29
1 Cor 5:7
1 Pet 1:19

1:30
Jn 1:15,27

1:32
Mt 3:16
Mk 1:10
Lk 3:22

1:33
Lk 3:16

1:34
Jn 1:49; 10:36

Jesus' First Disciples

35The next day John was there again with two of his disciples. 36When he saw Jesus passing by, he said, "Look, the Lamb of God!"

37When the two disciples heard him say this, they followed Jesus. 38Turning around, Jesus saw them following and asked, "What do you want?"

They said, "Rabbi" (which means Teacher), "where are you staying?"

39"Come," he replied, "and you will see."

So they went and saw where he was staying, and spent that day with him. It was about the tenth hour.

40Andrew, Simon Peter's brother, was one of the two who heard what John had said and who had followed Jesus. 41The first thing Andrew did was to find his brother Simon and tell him, "We have found the Messiah" (that is, the Christ). 42And he brought him to Jesus.

1:40
Mt 4:18-22
Mk 1:16
Lk 5:2-11

1:41
Job 23:3
Dan 9:25
Jn 4:25

1:42
Mt 16:18
1 Cor 15:5
1 Pet 2:5
Rev 21:14

● **1:29** Every morning and evening, a lamb was sacrificed in the temple for the sins of the people (Exodus 29:38–42). Isaiah 53:7 prophesied that the Messiah, God's servant, would be led to the slaughter like a lamb. To pay the penalty for sin, a life had to be given—and God chose to provide the sacrifice himself. The sins of the world were removed when Jesus died as the perfect sacrifice. This is the way our sins are forgiven (1 Corinthians 5:7). The "sin of the world" means everyone's sin, the sin of each individual. Jesus paid the price of *your* sin by his death. You can receive forgiveness by confessing your sin to him and asking for his forgiveness.

1:30 Although John the Baptist was a well-known preacher and attracted large crowds, he was content for Jesus to take the higher place. This is true humility, the basis for greatness in preaching, teaching, or any other work we do for Christ. When you are content to do what God wants you to do and let Jesus Christ be honored for it, God will do great things through you.

1:31–34 At Jesus' baptism, John the Baptist declared him the Messiah. At this time God gave John a sign to show him that Jesus was truly sent from God (1:33). John and Jesus were related, so John probably knew who he was. But it wasn't until his baptism that he understood Jesus to be the Messiah. Jesus' baptism is described in Matthew 3:13–17; Mark 1:9–11; and Luke 3:21, 22.

1:33 John the Baptist's baptism with water was preparatory because it was for repentance and symbolized the washing away of sins. Jesus, by contrast, would baptize with the Holy Spirit. He would send the Holy Spirit upon all believers, empowering them to live and teach the message of salvation. This began after Jesus had risen from the dead and ascended into heaven (see 20:22; Acts 2).

1:34 John the Baptist's job was to point people to Jesus, the Messiah for whom they were looking. Today people are looking for someone to give them security in an insecure world. Our job is to point them to Christ and to show that he is the one they seek.

● **1:35ff** These new disciples used several names for Jesus: Lamb of God (1:36), Rabbi (1:38), Messiah (1:41), Son of God (1:49), King of Israel (1:49). As they got to know Jesus, their appreciation for him grew. The more time we spend getting to know Christ, the more we understand and appreciate who he is. We may be drawn to him for his teaching, but we will come to know him as the Son of God. Although these disciples made this verbal shift in a few days, they would not fully understand until three years later (Acts 2). What they so easily professed had to be worked out in experience. We may find that words of faith come easily, but deep appreciation for Christ comes with living by faith.

● **1:37** One of the two disciples was Andrew (1:40). The other was probably John, the writer of this book. Why did these disciples leave John the Baptist? Because that's what John wanted them to do—he pointed the way to Jesus, whom he had prepared them to follow. These were Jesus' first disciples, along with Simon Peter (1:42) and Nathanael (1:45).

1:38 When the two disciples began to follow Jesus, he asked them, "What do you want?" Following Christ is not enough; we must follow him for the right reasons. To follow Christ for our own purposes is asking Christ to follow us—to align with us to build our cause, not his. We must examine our motives for following him. Are we seeking his glory or ours?

1:40 Andrew accepted John the Baptist's testimony about Jesus and immediately went to tell his brother, Simon, about him. There was no question in his mind that Jesus was the Messiah. Not only did he tell his brother, often Andrew was eager to introduce people to Jesus (see 6:8, 9; 12:22).

1:42 Jesus saw not only who Simon was, but who he would become. That is why he gave him a new name—Cephas in Greek, Peter in Latin (the name means "a rock"). Peter is not presented as rock-solid throughout the Gospels, but he became a solid rock in the days of the early church, as we learn in the book of Acts. By giving Simon a new name, Jesus introduced a change in character. For more on Simon Peter, see his Profile in Matthew 26.

Jesus looked at him and said, "You are Simon son of John. You will be called Cephas" (which, when translated, is Peter*ᵃ*).

Jesus Calls Philip and Nathanael

1:43
Jn 6:5,6
12:20-22

1:45
Gen 3:15; 26:4
49:10
Num 21:8,9
Deut 18:15,18
Ps 2; 16:8-11,22
110; 132:11
Isa 6:5; 7:14; 9:6
11:1-10; 32:1-5
42:1-9; 49:1-13
50:6,53
Jer 23:5,6
33:15
Ezek 34:23
37:25
Dan 7:13; 9:25
Mic 5:2
Zech 3:8,9
6:12; 9:9; 13:1,7

1:49
Jn 1:34

1:51
Gen 28:12

2:1
Jn 1:29,35,43

⁴³The next day Jesus decided to leave for Galilee. Finding Philip, he said to him, "Follow me."

⁴⁴Philip, like Andrew and Peter, was from the town of Bethsaida. ⁴⁵Philip found Nathanael and told him, "We have found the one Moses wrote about in the Law, and about whom the prophets also wrote—Jesus of Nazareth, the son of Joseph."

⁴⁶"Nazareth! Can anything good come from there?" Nathanael asked.

"Come and see," said Philip.

⁴⁷When Jesus saw Nathanael approaching, he said of him, "Here is a true Israelite, in whom there is nothing false."

⁴⁸"How do you know me?" Nathanael asked.

Jesus answered, "I saw you while you were still under the fig tree before Philip called you."

⁴⁹Then Nathanael declared, "Rabbi, you are the Son of God; you are the King of Israel."

⁵⁰Jesus said, "You believe*ᵇ* because I told you I saw you under the fig tree. You shall see greater things than that." ⁵¹He then added, "I tell you*ᶜ* the truth, you*ᶜ* shall see heaven open, and the angels of God ascending and descending on the Son of Man."

Jesus Changes Water to Wine

2 On the third day a wedding took place at Cana in Galilee. Jesus' mother was there, ²and Jesus and his disciples had also been invited to the wedding. ³When the wine was gone, Jesus' mother said to him, "They have no more wine."

ᵃ42 Both Cephas (Aramaic) and Peter (Greek) mean rock. ᵇ50 Or Do you believe . . . ? ᶜ51 The Greek is plural.

JESUS' FIRST TRAVELS
After his baptism by John in the Jordan River and temptation by Satan in the desert (see the map in Mark 1), Jesus returned to Galilee. He visited Nazareth, Cana, and Capernaum, and then returned to Jerusalem for the Passover.

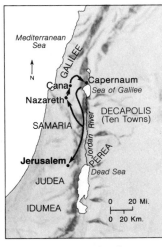

cause them to miss his power and love. Invite them to come and see who he really is.

1:47–49 Jesus knew about Nathanael before the two ever met. Christ also knows what we are really like. An honest person will feel comfortable with the thought that Jesus knows him through and through. A dishonest person will feel uncomfortable. You can't pretend to be something you're not. God knows the real you and wants *you* to follow him.

1:51 Jesus was referring to Jacob's dream recorded in Genesis 28:12. As the unique God-man, Jesus would be the ladder between heaven and earth. This would not be a physical experience such as the transfiguration, but spiritual insight into Jesus' true nature and purpose for coming.

2:1, 2 Jesus was on a mission to save the world, the greatest mission in the history of mankind. Yet he took time to attend a wedding and take part in its festivities. We may be tempted to think we should not take time out from our "important" work for social occasions. But maybe these social occasions are part of our mission. Jesus valued these wedding festivities because they involved people, and Jesus came to be with people. Our mission can often be accomplished in joyous times of celebration with others. Bring balance to your life by bringing Jesus into times of pleasure as well as times of work.

2:1–3 Weddings in Jesus' day were week-long festivals. Banquets were prepared for many guests, and the week was spent celebrating the new life of the married couple. Often the whole town was invited, and everybody came—it was considered an insult to refuse an invitation to a wedding. To accommodate many people, careful planning was needed. To run out of wine was more than embarrassing; it broke the strong unwritten laws of hospitality. Jesus was about to respond to a heartfelt need.

1:46 Nazareth was despised by the Jews because a Roman army garrison was located there. Nathanael's harsh comment reflected the common view. Nathanael's hometown was Cana, about four miles from Nazareth.

●**1:46** When Nathanael heard that the Messiah was from Nazareth, he was surprised. Philip responded, "Come and see." Fortunately, Nathanael went to meet Jesus and became a disciple. If he had acted on his prejudice without investigating further, he would have missed the Messiah! Don't let people's stereotypes about Christ

4"Dear woman, why do you involve me?" Jesus replied. "My time has not yet come."

2:4
Eccles 3:1
Mt 12:46-49
Jn 7:6; 8:20
19:26

5His mother said to the servants, "Do whatever he tells you."

6Nearby stood six stone water jars, the kind used by the Jews for ceremonial washing, each holding from twenty to thirty gallons. *a*

2:6
Mk 7:3,4
Jn 3:25

7Jesus said to the servants, "Fill the jars with water"; so they filled them to the brim.

8Then he told them, "Now draw some out and take it to the master of the banquet."

They did so, 9and the master of the banquet tasted the water that had been turned into wine. He did not realize where it had come from, though the servants who had drawn the water knew. Then he called the bridegroom aside 10and said, "Everyone brings out the choice wine first and then the cheaper wine after the guests have had too much to drink; but you have saved the best till now."

2:9
Jn 4:46

11This, the first of his miraculous signs, Jesus performed at Cana in Galilee. He thus revealed his glory, and his disciples put their faith in him.

2:11
Jn 2:23; 3:2
4:54; 6:14; 11:47
12:37

B. MESSAGE AND MINISTRY OF JESUS, THE SON OF GOD (2:12—12:50)

John stresses the deity of Christ. He gives us seven miracles that serve as signs that Jesus is the Messiah. In this section he records Jesus describing himself as the bread of life, the water of life, the light of the world, the door, and the good shepherd. John provides teachings of Jesus found nowhere else. This is the most theological of the four Gospels.

1. Jesus Encounters Belief and Unbelief From the People

Jesus Clears the Temple

12After this he went down to Capernaum with his mother and brothers and his disciples. There they stayed for a few days.

2:12
Mt 12:46-50

13When it was almost time for the Jewish Passover, Jesus went up to Jerusalem.

2:13
Ex 12:14

a6 Greek *two to three metretes* (probably about 75 to 115 liters)

2:4 Mary was probably not asking Jesus to do a miracle; she simply hoped her son would help solve this major problem and find some wine. Tradition says that Joseph, Mary's husband, was dead, so she probably was used to asking for her son's help in difficult situations. Jesus' answer to Mary is difficult to understand, but maybe that is the point. Although Mary did not understand what Jesus was going to do, she trusted him to do the right thing. Those who believe in Jesus but run into situations they cannot understand must continue to trust that he will work in the best way.

2:5 Mary submitted to Jesus' way of doing things. She recognized that Jesus was more than her human son—he was the Son of God. When we bring our problems to Christ, we may think we know how he should take care of them. But he may have a completely different plan. Like Mary, we should submit and allow him to deal with the problem as he sees best.

2:6 The six stone water jars were normally used for ceremonial washing. When full, the pots would hold 20 to 30 gallons. According to the Jews' ceremonial law, people became symbolically unclean by touching objects of everyday life. Before eating, they poured water over their hands to cleanse themselves of any bad influences associated with what they had touched.

2:10 People look everywhere but to God for excitement and meaning. They somehow expect God to be dull and lifeless. Just as the wine Jesus made was the best, so life in him is better than life on our own. Why wait until everything else runs out before trying God? Why save the best until last?

2:11 When the disciples saw Jesus' miracle, they believed. The miracle showed his power over nature and revealed the way he would go about his ministry—helping others, speaking with authority, and being in personal touch with people.

2:11 Miracles are not merely superhuman happenings, but happenings that demonstrate God's power. Almost every miracle Jesus did was a renewal of fallen creation—restoring sight, making the lame walk, even restoring life to the dead. Believe in him not because he is a superman but because he is God continuing his creation, even in those of us who are poor, weak, crippled, orphaned, blind, lame, or with some other desperate need for re-creation.

2:12 Capernaum became Jesus' home base during his ministry in Galilee. Located on a major trade route, it was an important city in the region, with a Roman garrison and a customs station. At Capernaum, Matthew was called to be a disciple (Matthew 9:9). The city was also the home of several other disciples (Matthew 4:13–19) and a high-ranking government official (4:46). It had at least one major synagogue. Although Jesus made this city his base of operations in Galilee, he condemned it for the people's unbelief (Matthew 11:23; Luke 10:15).

2:13 The Passover celebration took place yearly at the temple in Jerusalem. Every Jewish male was expected to make a pilgrimage to Jerusalem this time (Deuteronomy 16:16). This was a week-long festival—the Passover was one day, and the Feast of Unleavened Bread lasted the rest of the week. The entire week commemorated the freeing of the Jews from slavery in Egypt (Exodus 12:1–13).

2:13 Jerusalem was both the religious and the political seat of Palestine, and the place where the Messiah was expected to arrive. The temple was located there, and many Jewish families from all over the world traveled to Jerusalem during the key feasts. The temple was built on an imposing site, a hill overlooking the city. Solomon had built the first temple on this same site almost 1,000 years earlier (949 B.C.), but his temple was destroyed by the Bab-

¹⁴In the temple courts he found men selling cattle, sheep and doves, and others sitting at tables exchanging money. ¹⁵So he made a whip out of cords, and drove all from the temple area, both sheep and cattle; he scattered the coins of the money changers and overturned their tables. ¹⁶To those who sold doves he said, "Get these out of here! How dare you turn my Father's house into a market!"

¹⁷His disciples remembered that it is written: "Zeal for your house will consume me." *a*

¹⁸Then the Jews demanded of him, "What miraculous sign can you show us to prove your authority to do all this?"

¹⁹Jesus answered them, "Destroy this temple, and I will raise it again in three days."

²⁰The Jews replied, "It has taken forty-six years to build this temple, and you are going to raise it in three days?" ²¹But the temple he had spoken of was his body. ²²After he was raised from the dead, his disciples recalled what he had said. Then they believed the Scripture and the words that Jesus had spoken.

²³Now while he was in Jerusalem at the Passover Feast, many people saw the miraculous signs he was doing and believed in his name. *b* ²⁴But Jesus would not entrust himself to them, for he knew all men. ²⁵He did not need man's testimony about man, for he knew what was in a man.

a17 Psalm 69:9   *b23* Or *and believed in him*

2:16
Lk 2:49
Jn 14:2

2:17
Ps 69:9

2:18
Mt 12:38

2:19
Mt 26:61; 27:40
Mk 14:58
Acts 6:14

2:20
Ezra 5:16

2:21
Jn 10:38
14:2,10; 17:21
1 Cor 3:16; 6:19
2 Cor 6:16
Eph 2:21,22
Col 2:9
1 Pet 2:4-7

2:22
Ps 2:7; 16:10
Lk 24:8,25,26
Jn 12:16; 14:26

---

ylonians (2 Kings 25). The temple was rebuilt in 515 B.C., and Herod the Great enlarged and remodeled it.

2:14ff John records this first cleansing of the temple. A second cleansing occurred at the end of Jesus' ministry, about three years later, and is recorded in Matthew 21:12–17; Mark 11:12–19; Luke 19:45–48.

2:14 The temple area was always crowded during Passover with thousands of out-of-town visitors. The religious leaders crowded it even further by allowing money changers and merchants to set up booths in the court of the Gentiles. They rationalized this practice as a convenience for the worshipers and as a way to make money for temple upkeep. But the religious leaders did not seem to care that the court of the Gentiles was so full of merchants that foreigners found it difficult to worship. And worship was the main purpose for visiting the temple. No wonder Jesus was angry!

2:14 The temple tax had to be paid in local currency, so foreigners had to have their money changed. The money changers, unfortunately, often charged exorbitant exchange rates. The people were also required to make a sacrifice for sin. Because of the long journey, many could not bring their own animals. Some who brought animals had them rejected for imperfections. Thus animal merchants did a flourishing business in the temple courtyard. The price of sacrificial animals was much higher in the temple area than elsewhere. Jesus was angry at the dishonest, greedy practices of the money changers and merchants, and he particularly disliked their presence on the temple grounds. They made a mockery of God's house of worship.

2:14–16 God's temple was being misused by people who turned it into a marketplace. They forgot, or didn't care, that God's house is a place of worship, not a place for making a profit. Our attitude toward the church is wrong if we see it as a place for personal contacts or business advantage. Make sure you attend church to worship God.

2:15, 16 Jesus was obviously angry at the merchants who exploited those who had come to God's house to worship. There is a difference between uncontrolled rage and righteous indignation— yet both are called anger. We must be very careful how we use the powerful emotion of anger. It is right to be angry about injustice and sin; it is wrong to be angry over trivial personal offenses.

2:15, 16 Jesus made a whip and chased out the money changers. Does his example permit us to use violence against wrongdoers? Certain authority is granted to some, but not to all. For example, the authority to use weapons and restrain people is granted to police officers, but not to the general public. The authority to imprison people is granted to judges, but not to individual citizens. Jesus had God's authority, something we cannot have. While we want to live like Christ, we should never try to claim his authority where it has not been given to us.

2:17 Jesus took the evil acts in the temple as an insult against God, and thus he did not deal with them halfheartedly. He was consumed with righteous anger against such flagrant disrespect for God.

2:19, 20 The Jews understood Jesus to mean the temple out of which he had just driven the merchants and money changers. This was the temple Zerubbabel had built over 500 years earlier, but Herod the Great had begun remodeling it, making it much larger and far more beautiful. It had been 46 years since this remodeling had started (20 B.C.), and it still wasn't completely finished. They understood Jesus' words to mean that this imposing building could be torn down and rebuilt in three days, and they were startled.

2:21, 22 Jesus was not talking about the literal temple, but about himself. His listeners didn't realize it, but he was greater than the temple (Matthew 12:6). His words would take on meaning for his disciples after his resurrection. That Christ so perfectly fulfilled this prediction became the strongest proof for his claims to be God.

2:23–25 Jesus, the Son of God, knows all about human nature. He was well aware of the truth of Jeremiah 17:9, which states, "The heart is deceitful above all things and beyond cure. Who can understand it?" Jesus was discerning and he knew that the faith of some would-be followers was superficial. Some of the same people claiming to believe in Jesus at this time would later yell "Crucify him!" It's easy to believe when it is exciting and everyone else believes the same way. But keep your faith firm even when it isn't popular to believe.

Jesus Teaches Nicodemus

3 Now there was a man of the Pharisees named Nicodemus, a member of the Jewish ruling council. ²He came to Jesus at night and said, "Rabbi, we know you are a teacher who has come from God. For no one could perform the miraculous signs you are doing if God were not with him."

³In reply Jesus declared, "I tell you the truth, no one can see the kingdom of God unless he is born again. *a*"

⁴"How can a man be born when he is old?" Nicodemus asked. "Surely he cannot enter a second time into his mother's womb to be born!"

⁵Jesus answered, "I tell you the truth, no one can enter the kingdom of God unless he is born of water and the Spirit. ⁶Flesh gives birth to flesh, but the Spirit *b* gives birth to spirit. ⁷You should not be surprised at my saying, 'You *c* must be born again.' ⁸The wind blows wherever it pleases. You hear its sound, but you cannot tell where it comes from or where it is going. So it is with everyone born of the Spirit."

⁹"How can this be?" Nicodemus asked.

¹⁰"You are Israel's teacher," said Jesus, "and do you not understand these

a3 Or *born from above*; also in verse 7 *b6* Or *but spirit* *c7* The Greek is plural.

3:1 Jn 7:50; 19:39
3:2 Jn 9:33 Acts 2:22; 10:38
3:3 Jn 1:13 1 Pet 1:23
3:5 Acts 2:38 Tit 3:4,5 1 Pet 3:21
3:6 Jn 1:13 Rom 8:15,16 Gal 4:6
3:8 Ezek 37:5,9,10,14

● 3:1 Nicodemus was a ruler and a member of the Pharisees, a group of religious leaders whom Jesus and John the Baptist often criticized for being hypocrites (see the note on Matthew 3:7 for more on the Pharisees). Most Pharisees were intensely jealous of Jesus because he undermined their authority and challenged their views. But Nicodemus was searching, and he believed Jesus had some answers. A learned teacher himself, he came to Jesus to be taught. No matter how intelligent and well educated you are, you must come to Jesus with an open mind and heart so he can teach you the truth about God.

3:1ff Nicodemus came to Jesus personally although he could have sent one of his assistants. He wanted to examine Jesus for himself to separate fact from rumor. Perhaps he was afraid of what his peers, the Pharisees, would say about his visit, so he came after dark. Later, when he understood that Jesus was truly the Messiah, he spoke up boldly in his defense (7:50, 51). Like Nicodemus, we must examine Jesus for ourselves—others cannot do it for us. Then, if we believe he is who he says, we will want to speak up for him.

● 3:3 What did Nicodemus know about the kingdom? From the Bible he knew it would be ruled by God, it would be restored on earth, and it would incorporate God's people. Jesus revealed to this devout Pharisee that the kingdom would come to the whole world (3:16), not just the Jews, and that Nicodemus wouldn't be a part of it unless he was personally born again (3:5). This was a revolutionary concept: the kingdom is personal, not national or ethnic, and its entrance requirements are repentance and spiritual rebirth. Jesus later taught that God's kingdom has *already begun* in the hearts of believers. It will be fully realized when Jesus returns to judge the world and abolish evil forever (Revelation 21:22).

3:5, 6 "Of water and the Spirit" could be referring to (1) the contrast between physical birth (water) and spiritual birth (Spirit), or (2) being regenerated by the Spirit and demonstrating that rebirth by Christian baptism. The water may also represent the cleansing action of God's Holy Spirit (Titus 3:5). Nicodemus would have been familiar with God's promise in Ezekiel 36:25, 26. Jesus is explaining the importance of a spiritual rebirth, saying we don't enter the kingdom by living a better life, but by being spiritually reborn.

3:6 Who is the Holy Spirit? God is three persons in one—the Father, the Son, and the Holy Spirit. God became a man in Jesus so that Jesus could die for our sins. Jesus rose from the dead to offer salvation to all people through spiritual renewal and rebirth. When Jesus ascended into heaven, his physical presence left the earth, but he promised to send the Holy Spirit so his spiritual presence would still be among mankind (see Luke 24:49). The Holy Spirit first became available to all believers at Pentecost (Acts 2).

Whereas in Old Testament days the Holy Spirit empowered specific individuals for specific purposes, now all believers have the power of the Holy Spirit available to them. For more on the Holy Spirit, read 14:16–28; Romans 8:9; 1 Corinthians 12:13; and 2 Corinthians 1:22.

THE VISIT IN SAMARIA
Jesus went to Jerusalem for the Passover, cleared the temple, and talked with Nicodemus, a religious leader, about eternal life. He then left Jerusalem and traveled in Judea. On his way to Galilee, he visited Sychar and other villages in Samaria. Unlike most Jews of the day, he did not try to avoid the region of Samaria.

3:8 Jesus explained that we cannot control the work of the Holy Spirit. He works in ways we cannot predict or understand. Just as you did not control your physical birth, so you cannot control your spiritual birth. It is a gift from God through the Holy Spirit (Romans 8:16; 1 Corinthians 2:10–12; 1 Thessalonians 1:5, 6).

● 3:8 Are there people you disregard, thinking they could never be brought to God—such as a world leader for whom you have never prayed or a successful person to whom you have never witnessed? Don't assume that anyone is beyond the reach of the gospel. God, through his Holy Spirit, can reach anyone, and you should pray diligently for whomever he brings to your mind. Be a witness and example to everyone with whom you have contact. God may touch those you think most unlikely—and he may use , you to do it.

3:10, 11 This Jewish teacher of the Bible knew the Old Testament thoroughly, but he didn't understand what it said about the Messiah. Knowledge is not salvation. You should know the Bible; but

3:13
Jn 6:38,42
16:28
Rom 10:6
Eph 4:9,10
3:14
Num 21:8,9
3:15
1 Jn 5:11,12

things? 11I tell you the truth, we speak of what we know, and we testify to what we have seen, but still you people do not accept our testimony. 12I have spoken to you of earthly things and you do not believe; how then will you believe if I speak of heavenly things? 13No one has ever gone into heaven except the one who came from heaven—the Son of Man. *a* 14Just as Moses lifted up the snake in the desert, so the Son of Man must be lifted up, 15that everyone who believes in him may have eternal life. *b*

a13 Some manuscripts *Man, who is in heaven*   *b15* Or *believes may have eternal life in him*

NICODEMUS

God specializes in finding and changing people we consider out of reach. It took awhile for Nicodemus to come out of the dark, but God was patient with this "undercover" believer.

Afraid of being discovered, Nicodemus made an appointment to see Jesus at night. Daylight conversations between Pharisees and Jesus tended to be antagonistic, but Nicodemus really wanted to learn. He probably got a lot more than he expected—a challenge to a new life! We know very little about Nicodemus, but we know that he left that evening's encounter a changed man. He came away with a whole new understanding of both God and himself.

Nicodemus next appears as part of the Jewish council. As it discussed ways to eliminate Jesus, Nicodemus raised the question of justice. Although his objection was overruled, he had spoken up. He had begun to change.

Our last picture of Nicodemus shows him joining Joseph of Arimathea in asking for Jesus' body to bury. Realizing what he was risking, Nicodemus was making a bold move. He was continuing to grow.

God looks for steady growth, not instant perfection. How well does your present level of spiritual growth match up with how long you have known Jesus?

Strengths and accomplishments:
- One of the few religious leaders who believed in Jesus
- A member of the powerful ruling council
- A Pharisee who was attracted by Jesus' character and miracles
- Joined with Joseph of Arimathea in burying Jesus

Weakness and mistake:
- Limited by his fear of being publicly exposed as Jesus' follower

Lessons from his life:
- Unless we are born again, we can never be part of the kingdom of God
- God is able to change those we might consider unreachable
- God is patient, but persistent
- If we are available, God can use us

Vital statistics:
- Where: Jerusalem
- Occupation: Religious leader
- Contemporaries: Jesus, Annas, Caiaphas, Pilate, Joseph of Arimathea

Key verse:
" 'How can a man be born when he is old?' Nicodemus asked. 'Surely he cannot enter a second time into his mother's womb to be born!' " (John 3:4).

Nicodemus's story is told in John 3:1–21; 7:50–52; and 19:39, 40.

even more important, you should understand the God it reveals and the salvation he offers.

3:14, 15 When the Israelites were wandering in the wilderness, God sent a plague of snakes to punish the people for their rebellious attitudes. Those doomed to die from snakebite could be healed by obeying God's command to look up at the elevated bronze snake and by believing that God would heal them if they did (see Numbers 21:8, 9). Similarly, our salvation happens when we look up to Jesus, believing he will save us. God has provided this way for us to be healed of sin's deadly bite.

16"For God so loved the world that he gave his one and only Son, *a* that whoever believes in him shall not perish but have eternal life. 17For God did not send his Son into the world to condemn the world, but to save the world through him. 18Whoever believes in him is not condemned, but whoever does not believe stands condemned already because he has not believed in the name of God's one and only Son. *b* 19This is the verdict: Light has come into the world, but men loved darkness instead of light because their deeds were evil. 20Everyone who does evil hates the light, and will not come into the light for fear that his deeds will be exposed. 21But whoever lives by the truth comes into the light, so that it may be seen plainly that what he has done has been done through God." *c*

3:16
Rom 5:8; 8:32
3:17
Jn 12:47
3:18
Jn 5:24
3:19
Jn 1:4,5; 7:7
8:12; 12:46
3:20
Eph 5:11-13
3:21
1 Jn 1:7

John the Baptist's Testimony About Jesus

22After this, Jesus and his disciples went out into the Judean countryside, where he spent some time with them, and baptized. 23Now John also was baptizing at Aenon near Salim, because there was plenty of water, and people were constantly coming to be baptized. 24(This was before John was put in prison.) 25An argument developed between some of John's disciples and a certain Jew *d* over the matter of ceremonial washing. 26They came to John and said to him, "Rabbi, that man who was with you on the other side of the Jordan—the one you testified about—well, he is baptizing, and everyone is going to him."

27To this John replied, "A man can receive only what is given him from heaven. 28You yourselves can testify that I said, 'I am not the Christ *e* but am sent ahead of him.' 29The bride belongs to the bridegroom. The friend who attends the bridegroom waits and listens for him, and is full of joy when he hears the bridegroom's voice. That joy is mine, and it is now complete. 30He must become greater; I must become less.

3:22
Jn 4:2
3:24
Mt 4:12
3:26
Jn 1:6,7,34
3:27
1 Cor 4:7
Heb 5:4
3:28
Mal 3:1
Jn 1:20,23
3:29
Isa 62:5
2 Cor 11:2
Rev 21:9

a16 Or *his only begotten Son*   *b18* Or *God's only begotten Son*   *c21* Some interpreters end the quotation after verse 15.   *d25* Some manuscripts *and certain Jews*   *e28* Or *Messiah*

●3:16 The entire gospel comes to a focus in this verse. God's love is not static or self-centered; it reaches out and draws others in. Here God sets the pattern of true love, the basis for all love relationships—if you love someone dearly, you are willing to pay dearly for that person's responsive love. God paid dearly with the life of his Son, the highest price he could pay. Jesus accepted our punishment, paid the price for our sins, and then offered us the new life he bought for us. When we share the gospel with others, our love must be like his—willingly giving up our own comfort and security so that others might join us in receiving God's love.

●3:16 Some people are repulsed by the idea of eternal life because their lives are miserable. But eternal life is not an extension of man's miserable, mortal life; eternal life is God's life embodied in Christ given to all believers now as a guarantee that they will live forever. In eternal life there is no death, sickness, enemy, evil, or sin. When we don't know Christ, we make choices as though this life were all we had. In reality, this life is just the introduction to eternity. Receive this new life by faith and begin to evaluate all that happens from an eternal perspective.

●3:16 To believe is more than intellectual agreement that Jesus is God. It means to put our trust and confidence in him that he alone can save us. It is to put him in charge of our present plans and eternal destiny. Believing is both trusting his words as reliable, and relying on him for the power to change. If you have never trusted him, let this promise of everlasting life be yours.

3:18 People often try to protect themselves from their fears by putting their trust in something they do or have: their good works, their skill or intelligence, their money or possessions. But only God can save us from the one thing we really need to fear—eternal condemnation. We trust in God by recognizing the insufficiency of our own efforts to find salvation and by asking him to do his work in us. When Jesus talks about unbelievers, he means those who reject or ignore him completely, not those who have momentary doubts.

●3:19-21 Many people don't want their lives exposed to God's light because they are afraid of what it will reveal. They don't want to be changed. Don't be surprised when these same people are threatened by your desire to obey God and do what is right, because they are afraid that the light in you may expose some of the darkness in their lives. Rather than giving in to discouragement, keep praying that they will come to see how much better it is to live in light than in darkness.

●3:25ff Some people look for points of disagreement so they can sow seeds of discord, discontent, and doubt. John the Baptist ended this theological argument by focusing on his devotion to Christ. It is divisive to try to force others to believe our way. Instead, let's witness about what Christ has done for us. How can anyone argue with us about that?

●3:26 John the Baptist's disciples were disturbed because people were following Jesus instead of John. It is easy to grow jealous of the popularity of another person's ministry. But we must remember that our true mission is to influence people to follow Christ, not us.

3:27 Why did John the Baptist continue to baptize after Jesus came onto the scene? Why didn't he become a disciple too? John explained that God gave him his work, and he had to continue it until God called him to do something else. John's main purpose was to point people to Christ. Even with Jesus beginning his own ministry, John could still point people to him.

3:27 John believed God had appointed him. If God appoints us to a task, it becomes a high and holy privilege. We should accept it with great enthusiasm.

3:30 John's willingness to decrease in importance shows unusual humility. Pastors and other Christian leaders can be tempted to focus more on the success of their ministries than on Christ. Beware of those who put more emphasis on their own achievements than on God's kingdom.

3:32
Jn 3:11

3:33
1 Jn 5:10

3:34
Jn 6:63

3:35
Jn 5:20; 17:2,24

3:36
Jn 3:16

31"The one who comes from above is above all; the one who is from the earth belongs to the earth, and speaks as one from the earth. The one who comes from heaven is above all. 32He testifies to what he has seen and heard, but no one accepts his testimony. 33The man who has accepted it has certified that God is truthful. 34For the one whom God has sent speaks the words of God, for God*a* gives the Spirit without limit. 35The Father loves the Son and has placed everything in his hands. 36Whoever believes in the Son has eternal life, but whoever rejects the Son will not see life, for God's wrath remains on him."*b*

Jesus Talks With a Samaritan Woman

4 The Pharisees heard that Jesus was gaining and baptizing more disciples than John, 2although in fact it was not Jesus who baptized, but his disciples. 3When the Lord learned of this, he left Judea and went back once more to Galilee.

4:4
Lk 9:52

4:5,6
Gen 33:19
Josh 24:32

4:7
Gen 24:11

4:9
2 Kgs 17:24
Mt 10:5
Jn 8:48
Acts 10:48

4:10
Isa 12:3; 44:3
Jn 7:37-39
1 Cor 12:13
Rev 21:6; 22:17

4Now he had to go through Samaria. 5So he came to a town in Samaria called Sychar, near the plot of ground Jacob had given to his son Joseph. 6Jacob's well was there, and Jesus, tired as he was from the journey, sat down by the well. It was about the sixth hour.

7When a Samaritan woman came to draw water, Jesus said to her, "Will you give me a drink?" 8(His disciples had gone into the town to buy food.)

9The Samaritan woman said to him, "You are a Jew and I am a Samaritan woman. How can you ask me for a drink?" (For Jews do not associate with Samaritans. *c*)

10Jesus answered her, "If you knew the gift of God and who it is that asks you for a drink, you would have asked him and he would have given you living water."

11"Sir," the woman said, "you have nothing to draw with and the well is deep.

a34 Greek *he* *b36* Some interpreters end the quotation after verse 30.   *c9 Or do not use dishes Samaritans have used*

3:31-35 Jesus' testimony was trustworthy because he came from heaven and spoke of what he saw there. His words were the very words of God. Your whole spiritual life depends on your answer to one question, "Who is Jesus Christ?" If you accept Jesus as only a prophet or teacher, you have to reject his teaching, for he claimed to be God's Son, even God himself. The heartbeat of John's Gospel is the dynamic truth that Jesus Christ is God's Son, the Messiah, the Savior, who was from the beginning and will continue to live forever. This same Jesus has invited us to accept him and live with him eternally. When we understand who Jesus is; we are compelled to believe what he said.

3:34 God's Spirit was upon Jesus without limit or measure. Thus Jesus was the highest revelation of God to man (Hebrews 1:2).

3:36 Jesus says that those who believe in him *have* (not *will* have) everlasting life. To receive eternal life is to join in God's life, which by nature is eternal. Thus, eternal life begins at the moment of spiritual rebirth.

3:36 The author of the Gospel of John has been demonstrating that Jesus is the true Son of God. He sets before us the greatest choice of life. We are responsible to decide today whom we will obey (Joshua 24:15), and God wants us to choose him and life (Deuteronomy 30:15-20). The wrath of God is God's final judgment and rejection of the sinner. To put off the choice is to choose not to follow Christ. Indecision is a fatal decision.

4:1-3 Already opposition was rising against Jesus, especially from the Pharisees. They resented Jesus' popularity as well as his message, which challenged much of their teachings. Because Jesus was just beginning his ministry, it wasn't yet time to confront these leaders openly, so he left Jerusalem and traveled north toward Galilee.

●**4:4** When the northern kingdom with its capital at Samaria fell to the Assyrians, many Jews were deported to Assyria, and foreigners were brought in to settle the land and help keep the peace (2 Kings 17:24). The intermarriage between those foreigners and

the remaining Jews resulted in a mixed race, impure in the opinion of Jews who lived in the southern kingdom. Thus the pure Jews hated this mixed race called Samaritans because they felt they had betrayed their people and nation. They set up an alternate center for worship on Mount Gerazim (4:20) to parallel the temple at Jerusalem; but it had been destroyed 150 years earlier. The Jews did everything they could to avoid traveling through Samaria. But Jesus had no reason to live by such cultural restrictions. The route through Samaria was shorter, and that was the route he took.

●**4:5-7** Jacob's well was on the property originally owned by Jacob. It was not a spring-fed well, but a well into which water seeped from rain and dew, collecting at the bottom. Wells were almost always located outside the city along the main road. Twice each day, morning and evening, women came to draw water. This woman came at noon, however, probably to avoid meeting people because of her reputation. Jesus gave this woman an extraordinary message about fresh and pure water that would quench her spiritual thirst forever.

4:7-9 This woman (1) was a Samaritan, a member of the hated mixed race, (2) was known to be living in sin, and (3) was in a public place. No respectable Jewish man would talk to a woman under such circumstances. But Jesus did. The gospel is for every person, no matter what his or her race, social position, or past sins. We must be prepared to share this gospel at any time in any place. Jesus crossed all barriers to share the gospel, and we who follow him must do no less.

4:10 What did Jesus mean by "living water"? In the Old Testament, many verses speak of thirsting after God as one thirsts for water (Psalm 42:1; Isaiah 55:1; Jeremiah 2:13; Zechariah 13:1). God is called the fountain of life (Psalm 36:9) and the spring of living water (Jeremiah 17:13). In saying he would bring living water that could forever quench one's thirst for God, Jesus was claiming to be the Messiah. Only the Messiah could give this gift that satisfies the soul's desire.

Where can you get this living water? 12Are you greater than our father Jacob, who gave us the well and drank from it himself, as did also his sons and his flocks and herds?"

13Jesus answered, "Everyone who drinks this water will be thirsty again, 14but whoever drinks the water I give him will never thirst. Indeed, the water I give him will become in him a spring of water welling up to eternal life."

4:14
Jn 6:35
7:37,38

15The woman said to him, "Sir, give me this water so that I won't get thirsty and have to keep coming here to draw water."

4:15
Jn 6:34

16He told her, "Go, call your husband and come back."

4:19
Lk 7:16

17"I have no husband," she replied.

Jesus said to her, "You are right when you say you have no husband. 18The fact is, you have had five husbands, and the man you now have is not your husband. What you have just said is quite true."

4:20
Gen 12:6,7
33:18
Judg 9:7
Deut 12:5
2 Chron 7:12

19"Sir," the woman said, "I can see that you are a prophet. 20Our fathers worshiped on this mountain, but you Jews claim that the place where we must worship is in Jerusalem."

4:21
Mal 1:11
1 Tim 2:8

21Jesus declared, "Believe me, woman, a time is coming when you will worship the Father neither on this mountain nor in Jerusalem. 22You Samaritans worship what you do not know; we worship what we do know, for salvation is from the Jews. 23Yet a time is coming and has now come when the true worshipers will worship the Father in spirit and truth, for they are the kind of worshipers the Father seeks. 24God is spirit, and his worshipers must worship in spirit and in truth."

4:22
2 Kings 17:28-41
Isa 2:3
Acts 17:24-29
Rom 3:1,2
9:4,5

4:23,24
2 Cor 3:17,18
Phil 3:3

25The woman said, "I know that Messiah" (called Christ) "is coming. When he comes, he will explain everything to us."

4:25
Deut 18:15

26Then Jesus declared, "I who speak to you am he."

4:26
Mk 14:61,62
Jn 8:24; 9:35-37

The Disciples Rejoin Jesus

27Just then his disciples returned and were surprised to find him talking with a woman. But no one asked, "What do you want?" or "Why are you talking with her?"

28Then, leaving her water jar, the woman went back to the town and said to the people, 29"Come, see a man who told me everything I ever did. Could this be the Christ*a*?" 30They came out of the town and made their way toward him.

4:29
Jn 7:26,31

31Meanwhile his disciples urged him, "Rabbi, eat something."

a29 Or Messiah

4:13–15 Many spiritual functions parallel physical functions. As our bodies hunger and thirst, so do our souls. But our souls need *spiritual* food and water. The woman confused the two kinds of water, perhaps because no one had ever talked with her about her spiritual hunger and thirst before. We would not think of depriving our bodies of food and water when they hunger or thirst. Why then should we deprive our souls? The living Word, Jesus Christ, and the written Word, the Bible, can satisfy our hungry and thirsty souls.

4:15 The woman mistakenly believed that if she received the water Jesus offered, she would not have to return to the well each day. She was interested in Jesus' message because she thought it could make her life easier. But if that were always the case, people would accept Christ's message for the wrong reasons. Christ did not come to take away challenges, but to change us on the inside and to empower us to deal with problems from God's perspective.

4:15 The woman did not immediately understand what Jesus was talking about. It takes time to accept something that changes the very foundations of your life. Jesus allowed the woman time to ask questions and put pieces together for herself. Sharing the gospel does not always have immediate results. When you ask people to let Jesus change their lives, give them time to weigh the matter.

4:16–20 When this woman discovered that Jesus knew all about her private life, she quickly changed the subject. Often people become uncomfortable when the conversation is too close to home,

and they try to change the subject. As we witness we should gently guide the conversation back to Christ. His presence reveals sin and makes people squirm, but only he can forgive the sins and give new life.

4:20–24 The woman brought up a popular theological issue—the correct place to worship. But her question was a smokescreen to keep Jesus away from her deepest need. Jesus directed the conversation to a much more important point: the *location* of worship is not nearly so important as the *attitude* of the worshipers.

4:21–24 "God is spirit" means he is not a physical being limited to one place. He is present everywhere and he can be worshiped anywhere, anytime. It is not where we worship that counts, but how we worship. Is your worship genuine and real? Do you have the Holy Spirit's help? How does the Holy Spirit help us worship? The Holy Spirit prays for us (Romans 8:26), teaches us the words of Christ (14:26), and tells us we are loved (Romans 5:5).

4:22 When Jesus said, "salvation is from the Jews," he meant that only through the Jewish Messiah would the whole world find salvation. God promised that through the Jewish race the whole earth would be blessed (Genesis 12:3). The Old Testament prophets called the Jews to be a light to the other nations of the world, bringing them to a knowledge of God; and they predicted the Messiah's coming. The woman at the well knew of these passages and was expecting the Messiah, but she didn't realize she was talking to him!

4:34
Job 23:12
Jn 5:30,36
6:38; 17:4
19:28,30

4:35
Mt 9:37,38
Lk 10:2

4:36
Dan 12:3
1 Cor 3:8,9
9:17-19

4:37
Job 31:8
Mic 6:15

4:42
Isa 49:6
Mt 1:21
Lk 2:29-31
Jn 1:29; 17:8
Acts 5:31; 13:23
Eph 2:13
Phil 3:20
1 Tim 1:15
1 Jn 4:14

4:43,44
Mt 13:57
Mk 6:4
Lk 4:24

4:45
Deut 16:16

4:46
Jn 2:1,11,23

4:48
1 Cor 1:22
Heb 2:4

32But he said to them, "I have food to eat that you know nothing about."

33Then his disciples said to each other, "Could someone have brought him food?"

34"My food," said Jesus, "is to do the will of him who sent me and to finish his work. 35Do you not say, 'Four months more and then the harvest'? I tell you, open your eyes and look at the fields! They are ripe for harvest. 36Even now the reaper draws his wages, even now he harvests the crop for eternal life, so that the sower and the reaper may be glad together. 37Thus the saying 'One sows and another reaps' is true. 38I sent you to reap what you have not worked for. Others have done the hard work, and you have reaped the benefits of their labor."

Many Samaritans Believe

39Many of the Samaritans from that town believed in him because of the woman's testimony, "He told me everything I ever did." 40So when the Samaritans came to him, they urged him to stay with them, and he stayed two days. 41And because of his words many more became believers.

42They said to the woman, "We no longer believe just because of what you said; now we have heard for ourselves, and we know that this man really is the Savior of the world."

Jesus Heals the Official's Son

43After the two days he left for Galilee. 44(Now Jesus himself had pointed out that a prophet has no honor in his own country.) 45When he arrived in Galilee, the Galileans welcomed him. They had seen all that he had done in Jerusalem at the Passover Feast, for they also had been there.

46Once more he visited Cana in Galilee, where he had turned the water into wine. And there was a certain royal official whose son lay sick at Capernaum. 47When this man heard that Jesus had arrived in Galilee from Judea, he went to him and begged him to come and heal his son, who was close to death.

48"Unless you people see miraculous signs and wonders," Jesus told him, "you will never believe."

49The royal official said, "Sir, come down before my child dies."

4:34 The "food" about which Jesus was speaking was his spiritual nourishment. It includes more than Bible study, prayer, and attending church. Spiritual nourishment also comes from doing God's will and helping to bring his work of salvation to completion. We are nourished not only by what we take in, but also by what we give out for God. In 17:4, Jesus refers to completing his work on earth.

4:35 Sometimes Christians excuse themselves from witnessing by saying their family or friends aren't ready to believe. Jesus, however, makes it clear that around us a continual harvest waits to be reaped. Don't let Jesus find you making excuses. Look around. You will find people ready to hear God's Word.

4:36-38 The wages Jesus offers are the joy of working for him and seeing the harvest of believers. These wages come to sower and reaper alike, because both find joy in seeing new believers come into Christ's kingdom. The phrase "others have done the hard work" (4:38) may refer to the Old Testament prophets and John the Baptist, who paved the way for the gospel.

4:39 The Samaritan woman immediately shared her experience with others. Despite her reputation, many took her invitation and came out to meet Jesus. Perhaps there are sins in our past of which we're ashamed. But Christ changes us. As people see these changes, they become curious. Use these opportunities to introduce them to Christ.

4:46-49 This royal official was probably an officer in Herod's service. He walked 20 miles to see Jesus and addressed him as "Sir," putting himself under Jesus even though he had legal authority over Jesus.

4:48 This miracle was more than a favor to one official; it was a

sign to all the people. John's Gospel was written to all mankind to urge faith in Christ. Here a government official had faith that Jesus could do what he claimed. He believed; *then* he saw.

JESUS RETURNS TO GALILEE

Jesus stayed in Sychar for two days, then went on to Galilee. He visited Nazareth and various towns in Galilee before arriving in Cana. From there he spoke the word of healing, and a government official's son in Capernaum was healed. The Gospel of Matthew tells us Jesus then settled in Capernaum (Matthew 4:12, 13).

⁵⁰Jesus replied, "You may go. Your son will live."

The man took Jesus at his word and departed. ⁵¹While he was still on the way, his servants met him with the news that his boy was living. ⁵²When he inquired as to the time when his son got better, they said to him, "The fever left him yesterday at the seventh hour."

⁵³Then the father realized that this was the exact time at which Jesus had said to him, "Your son will live." So he and all his household believed.

⁵⁴This was the second miraculous sign that Jesus performed, having come from Judea to Galilee.

4:53
Acts 11:14
16:34

4:54
Jn 2:11

The Healing at the Pool

5 Some time later, Jesus went up to Jerusalem for a feast of the Jews. ²Now there is in Jerusalem near the Sheep Gate a pool, which in Aramaic is called Bethesda*ᵃ* and which is surrounded by five covered colonnades. ³Here a great number of disabled people used to lie—the blind, the lame, the paralyzed. *ᵇ* ⁵One who was there had been an invalid for thirty-eight years. ⁶When Jesus saw him lying there and learned that he had been in this condition for a long time, he asked him, "Do you want to get well?"

⁷"Sir," the invalid replied, "I have no one to help me into the pool when the water is stirred. While I am trying to get in, someone else goes down ahead of me."

⁸Then Jesus said to him, "Get up! Pick up your mat and walk." ⁹At once the man was cured; he picked up his mat and walked.

The day on which this took place was a Sabbath, ¹⁰and so the Jews said to the man who had been healed, "It is the Sabbath; the law forbids you to carry your mat."

5:1
Lev 23:1,2
Deut 16:1
Jn 2:13

5:2
Neh 3:1; 12:39

5:6
Ps 72:13
113:5,6
Heb 4:13

5:8
Mt 9:6
Mk 2:11
Lk 5:24

5:10
Ex 20:10
Neh 13:19
Jer 17:21
Mt 12:2
Mk 2:24; 3:4
Lk 6:2; 13:14

ᵃ2 Some manuscripts Bethzatha; other manuscripts Bethsaida ᵇ3 Some less important manuscripts paralyzed—and they waited for the moving of the waters. ⁴From time to time an angel of the Lord would come down and stir up the waters. The first one into the pool after each such disturbance would be cured of whatever disease he had.

●4:50 This government official not only believed Jesus could heal; he also obeyed Jesus by returning home, thus demonstrating his faith. It isn't enough for us to say we believe Jesus can take care of our problems. We need to act as if he can. When you pray about a need or problem, live as though you believe Jesus can do what he says.

●4:51 Jesus' miracles were not mere illusions, the product of wishful thinking. Although the official's son was 20 miles away, he was healed when Jesus spoke the word. Distance was no problem because Christ has mastery over space. We can never put so much space between ourselves and Christ that he can no longer help us.

4:53 Notice how the official's faith grew. First, he believed enough to ask Jesus to help his son. Second, he believed Jesus' assurance that his son would live, and he acted on it. Third, he and his whole house believed in Jesus. Faith grows as we use it.

5:1 Three feasts required all Jewish males to come to Jerusalem: (1) the Feast of Passover and Unleavened Bread, (2) the Feast of Weeks (also called Pentecost), and (3) the Feast of Tabernacles.

5:3, 4 It is unclear whether an angel actually disturbed the water, or if this was just what the people believed. In either case, Jesus healed a man who had been waiting for 38 years to be healed.

5:6 After 38 years this man's problem had become a way of life. No one had ever helped him. He had no hope of ever being healed and no desire to help himself. His situation looked hopeless. But no matter how trapped you feel in your infirmities, God can minister to your deepest needs. Don't let a problem or hardship cause you to lose hope. God may have special work for you to do in spite of your condition, or even because of it. Many have ministered effectively to hurting people because they have triumphed over their own hurts.

●5:10 According to the Pharisees, carrying a mat on the Sabbath was work and was therefore unlawful. It did not break an Old Testament law, but the Pharisees' interpretation of God's command to "remember the Sabbath day by keeping it holy" (Exodus 20:8). This was just one of hundreds of rules they had added to the Old Testament law.

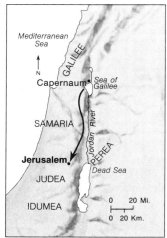

Mediterranean Sea
GALILEE
N
Capernaum • Sea of Galilee
SAMARIA
Jordan River
Jerusalem •
Dead Sea
JUDEA
PEREA
IDUMEA
0   20 Mi.
0   20 Km.

JESUS TEACHES IN JERUSALEM
Between chapters four and five of John, Jesus ministered throughout Galilee, especially in Capernaum. He had been calling certain men to follow him, but it wasn't until after this trip to Jerusalem (5:1) that he chose his 12 disciples from among them.

●5:10 A man who hadn't walked for 38 years was healed, but the Pharisees were more concerned about their petty rules than the life and health of a human being. It is easy to get so caught up in our man-made structures and rules that we forget the people involved. Are your guidelines for living God-made or man-made? Are they helping people, or have they become needless stumbling blocks?

11But he replied, "The man who made me well said to me, 'Pick up your mat and walk.' "

12So they asked him, "Who is this fellow who told you to pick it up and walk?"

13The man who was healed had no idea who it was, for Jesus had slipped away into the crowd that was there.

5:14
Jn 8:11

14Later Jesus found him at the temple and said to him, "See, you are well again. Stop sinning or something worse may happen to you." 15The man went away and told the Jews that it was Jesus who had made him well.

Life Through the Son

16So, because Jesus was doing these things on the Sabbath, the Jews persecuted

5:17
Jn 9:4; 14:10

him. 17Jesus said to them, "My Father is always at his work to this very day, and I, too, am working." 18For this reason the Jews tried all the harder to kill him; not

5:18
Jn 1:1,18
10:30,33; 20:28
Phil 2:6
Tit 2:13
2 Pet 1:1

only was he breaking the Sabbath, but he was even calling God his own Father, making himself equal with God.

5:19
Jn 8:28; 12:49

19Jesus gave them this answer: "I tell you the truth, the Son can do nothing by himself; he can do only what he sees his Father doing, because whatever the Father does the Son also does. 20For the Father loves the Son and shows him all he does. Yes, to your amazement he will show him even greater things than these. 21For just

THE CLAIMS OF CHRIST	Jesus claimed to be:	Matthew	Mark	Luke	John
Those who read the life of Christ are faced with one unavoidable question—was Jesus God? Part of any reasonable conclusion has to include the fact that he did claim to be God. We have no other choice but to agree or disagree with his claim. Eternal life is at stake in the choice.	the fulfillment of Old Testament prophecies	5:17; 14:33; 16:16, 17; 26:31, 53–56; 27:43	14:21, 61, 62	4:16–21; 7:18–23; 18:31; 22:37; 24:44	2:22; 5:45–47; 6:45; 7:40; 10:34–36; 13:18; 15:25; 20:9
	the Son of Man	8:20; 12:8; 16:27; 19:28; 20:18, 19; 24:27, 44; 25:31; 26:2, 45, 64	8:31, 38; 9:9; 10:45; 14:41	6:22; 7:33, 34; 12:8; 17:22; 18:8, 31; 19:10; 21:36	1:51; 3:13, 14; 6:27, 53; 12:23, 34
	the Son of God	11:27; 14:33; 16:16, 17; 27:43	3:11, 12	8:28; 10:22	1:18; 3:35, 36; 5:18–26; 6:40; 10:36; 11:4; 17:1; 19:7
	the Messiah/ the Christ	23:9, 10; 26:63, 64	8:29, 30	4:41; 23:1, 2; 24:25–27	4:25, 26; 10:24, 25; 11:27
	Teacher/Master	26:18			13:13, 14
	One with authority to forgive		2:1–12	7:48, 49	
	Lord		5:19		13:13, 14; 20:28
	Savior			19:10	3:17; 10:9

5:14 This man had been lame, or paralyzed, but now he could walk. This was a great miracle. But he needed an even greater miracle—to have his sins forgiven. The man was delighted to be physically healed, but he had to turn from his sins and seek God's forgiveness to be spiritually healed. God's forgiveness is the greatest gift you will ever receive. Don't neglect his gracious offer.

5:16 The Jewish leaders saw a mighty miracle of healing and a broken rule. They threw the miracle aside as they focused their attention on the broken rule, for the rule was more important to them than the miracle. God is prepared to work in our lives, but we can shut out his miracles by limiting our views about how he works.

5:17 If God stopped every kind of work on the Sabbath, nature would fall into chaos and sin would overrun the world. Genesis 2:2 says that God rested on the seventh day, but this can't mean he stopped doing good. Jesus wanted to teach that when the oppor-

tunity to do good presents itself, it should not be ignored, even on the Sabbath.

● **5:17ff** Jesus was identifying himself with God, his Father. There could be no doubt as to his claim to be God. Jesus does not leave us the option to believe in God while ignoring Jesus (5:23). The Pharisees also called God their Father, but they realized Jesus was claiming a unique relationship with him. In response to Jesus' claim, the Pharisees had two choices: to believe him, or to accuse him of blasphemy. They chose the second.

5:19-23 Because of his unity with God, Jesus lived as God wanted him to live. Because of our identification with Jesus, we must honor him and live as he wants us to live. The questions "What would Jesus do?" and "What would Jesus have me do?" may help us make the right choices.

as the Father raises the dead and gives them life, even so the Son gives life to whom he is pleased to give it. 22Moreover, the Father judges no one, but has entrusted all judgment to the Son, 23that all may honor the Son just as they honor the Father. He who does not honor the Son does not honor the Father, who sent him.

24"I tell you the truth, whoever hears my word and believes him who sent me has eternal life and will not be condemned; he has crossed over from death to life. 25I tell you the truth, a time is coming and has now come when the dead will hear the voice of the Son of God and those who hear will live. 26For as the Father has life in himself, so he has granted the Son to have life in himself. 27And he has given him authority to judge because he is the Son of Man.

28"Do not be amazed at this, for a time is coming when all who are in their graves will hear his voice 29and come out—those who have done good will rise to live, and those who have done evil will rise to be condemned. 30By myself I can do nothing; I judge only as I hear, and my judgment is just, for I seek not to please myself but him who sent me.

Testimonies About Jesus

31"If I testify about myself, my testimony is not valid. 32There is another who testifies in my favor, and I know that his testimony about me is valid.

33"You have sent to John and he has testified to the truth. 34Not that I accept human testimony; but I mention it that you may be saved. 35John was a lamp that burned and gave light, and you chose for a time to enjoy his light.

36"I have testimony weightier than that of John. For the very work that the Father has given me to finish, and which I am doing, testifies that the Father has sent me. 37And the Father who sent me has himself testified concerning me. You have never heard his voice nor seen his form, 38nor does his word dwell in you, for you do not believe the one he sent. 39You diligently study^a the Scriptures because you think that by them you possess eternal life. These are the Scriptures that testify about me, 40yet you refuse to come to me to have life.

41"I do not accept praise from men, 42but I know you. I know that you do not have the love of God in your hearts. 43I have come in my Father's name, and you do not accept me; but if someone else comes in his own name, you will accept him. 44How can you believe if you accept praise from one another, yet make no effort to obtain the praise that comes from the only God^b?

45"But do not think I will accuse you before the Father. Your accuser is Moses,

a39 Or Study diligently (the imperative)   b44 Some early manuscripts the Only One

5:21 Jn 11:25
5:23 1 Jn 2:23
5:24 Jn 20:30,31; 1 Jn 3:14; 5:13
5:25 Jn 4:21; 6:63,68
5:26 Jn 1:4; 6:57; 1 Jn 5:11,12
5:27 Dan 7:13,14; Acts 10:42; 17:31
5:29 Dan 12:2; Mt 25:31-46
5:30 Jn 5:19; 6:38
5:31 Jn 8:14
5:32 Jn 1:6,7,15
5:36 Jn 10:25,37,38; 14:11; 15:24; 1 Jn 5:9
5:37 Jn 1:18; 8:18
5:38 Jn 8:37; 1 Jn 2:14
5:39 Isa 34:16; Lk 16:29; 24:25; Jn 5:46,47; 7:52; Acts 13:27
5:41 Jn 7:18
5:45 Jn 9:28

5:24 Everlasting life—living forever with God—begins when you accept Jesus Christ as Savior. At that moment, new life begins in you (2 Corinthians 5:17). It is a completed transaction. You still face physical death, but when Christ returns again, your body will be resurrected to live forever.

5:25 In saying that the dead would hear his voice, Jesus was talking about the spiritually dead who hear, understand, and accept him. Those who accept God's Word will have eternal life. He was also talking about the physically dead. He raised several dead people while he was on earth, and at his second coming all the "dead in Christ" will rise to meet him (1 Thessalonians 4:16).

5:26 God is the source and Creator of life, for there is no life apart from God, here or hereafter. The life in us is a gift from him (see Deuteronomy 30:20; Psalm 36:9). Because Jesus is eternally existent with God, the Creator, he too is "the life" (14:6) through whom we may live eternally (see 1 John 5:11).

5:27 The Old Testament mentioned three signs of the coming Messiah. In this chapter, John shows that Jesus has fulfilled all three signs. All power and dominion are given to him as the Son of Man (cf. 5:27 with Daniel 7:13, 14). The lame and sick are healed (cf. 5:20, 26 with Isaiah 35:6; Jeremiah 31:8, 9). The dead are raised to life (cf. 5:21, 28 with Deuteronomy 32:39; 1 Samuel 2:6; 2 Kings 5:7).

5:29 Those who have rebelled against Christ will be resurrected too, but to hear God's judgment against them and to be sentenced to eternity apart from him. There are those who wish to live well on earth, ignore God, and see death as final rest. Jesus does not allow unbelieving people to see death as the end of it all. There is a judgment to face.

5:31ff Jesus claimed to be equal with God (5:18), to give eternal life (5:24), to be the source of life (5:26), and to judge sin (5:27). These statements make it clear that Jesus claimed to be divine— an almost unbelievable claim, but one that was supported by another witness, John the Baptist.

5:39, 40 The religious leaders knew what the Bible said but failed to apply its words to their lives. They knew the teachings of the Scriptures but failed to see the Messiah to whom the Scriptures pointed. They knew the rules but missed the Savior. Entrenched in their own religious system, they refused to let the Son of God change their lives.

5:41 Whose approval do you seek? The religious leaders enjoyed great prestige in Israel, but their stamp of approval meant nothing to Jesus. He was concerned about God's approval. This is a good principle for us. If even the highest officials in the world approve of our actions and God does not, we should be concerned. But if God approves, even though others don't, we should be content.

5:46
Gen 3:15; 12:3
18:18; 22:18
Deut 18:15,18

on whom your hopes are set. ⁴⁶If you believed Moses, you would believe me, for he wrote about me. ⁴⁷But since you do not believe what he wrote, how are you going to believe what I say?"

Jesus Feeds the Five Thousand

6:2
Mt 14:14
Mk 6:35
Lk 9:12

6 Some time after this, Jesus crossed to the far shore of the Sea of Galilee (that is, the Sea of Tiberias), ²and a great crowd of people followed him because they saw the miraculous signs he had performed on the sick. ³Then Jesus went up on a mountainside and sat down with his disciples. ⁴The Jewish Passover Feast was near.

6:6
Num 11:21,22

⁵When Jesus looked up and saw a great crowd coming toward him, he said to Philip, "Where shall we buy bread for these people to eat?" ⁶He asked this only to test him, for he already had in mind what he was going to do.

6:7
Mk 6:37

⁷Philip answered him, "Eight months' wages*a* would not buy enough bread for each one to have a bite!"

6:9
2 Kgs 4:43,44

⁸Another of his disciples, Andrew, Simon Peter's brother, spoke up, ⁹"Here is a boy with five small barley loaves and two small fish, but how far will they go among so many?"

6:10
Mt 14:21
Mk 6:43,44
6:11
1 Tim 4:4,5

¹⁰Jesus said, "Have the people sit down." There was plenty of grass in that place, and the men sat down, about five thousand of them. ¹¹Jesus then took the loaves, gave thanks, and distributed to those who were seated as much as they wanted. He did the same with the fish.

6:14
Gen 49:10
Deut 18:15,18
Isa 7:14; 9:6
Mt 11:3
Jn 1:21; 7:40-42

¹²When they had all had enough to eat, he said to his disciples, "Gather the pieces that are left over. Let nothing be wasted." ¹³So they gathered them and filled twelve baskets with the pieces of the five barley loaves left over by those who had eaten.

¹⁴After the people saw the miraculous sign that Jesus did, they began to say, "Surely this is the Prophet who is to come into the world." ¹⁵Jesus, knowing that

a7 Greek two hundred denarii

●5:45 The Pharisees prided themselves on being the true followers of their ancestor Moses. They followed every one of his laws to the letter and even added some of their own. Jesus' warning that Moses would accuse them stung them to fury. Moses wrote about Jesus (Genesis 3:15; Numbers 21:9; 24:17; Deuteronomy 18:15), yet the religious leaders refused to believe Jesus when he came.

6:5 If anyone knew where to get food, it would have been Philip, because he was from Bethsaida, a town about nine miles away (1:44). Jesus was testing him to strengthen his faith. By asking for a human solution (knowing that there was none), Jesus highlighted the powerful and miraculous act he was about to perform.

●6:5–7 Jesus asked Philip where they could buy a great amount of bread. Philip started assessing the probable cost. Jesus wanted to teach him that financial resources are not the most important ones. We can limit what God does in us by assuming what is and is not possible. Is there some impossible task you feel God wants you to do? Don't let your estimate of what can't be done keep you from taking on the task. God can do the miraculous; trust him to provide the resources.

6:8, 9 The disciples are contrasted with the youngster who brought what he had. They certainly had more resources than he did, but they knew they didn't have enough, so they didn't give anything at all. The boy gave what little he had, and it made all the difference. If we offer nothing to God, he will have nothing to use. But he can take what little we have and turn it into something great.

6:8, 9 In performing his miracles, Jesus usually preferred to work through people. Here he took what a young child offered and used it to accomplish one of the most spectacular miracles recorded in the Gospels. Age is no barrier to Christ. Never feel you are too young or old to be of service to him.

●6:13 There is a lesson in the leftovers. God gives in abundance.

He takes whatever we can offer him in time, ability, or resources and multiplies its effectiveness beyond our wildest expectations. If you take the first step in making yourself available to him, he will show you how greatly you can be used to advance the work of his kingdom.

JESUS WALKS ON THE WATER Jesus fed the 5,000 on a hillside near the Sea of Galilee at Bethsaida. The disciples set out across the sea toward Bethsaida or Capernaum. But they encountered a storm—and Jesus came walking to them on the water! The boat landed at Gennesaret (Mark 6:53). From there they went back to Capernaum.

6:14 "The Prophet" is the one prophesied by Moses (Deuteronomy 18:15).

they intended to come and make him king by force, withdrew again to a mountain by himself.

Jesus Walks on the Water

16When evening came, his disciples went down to the lake, 17where they got into a boat and set off across the lake for Capernaum. By now it was dark, and Jesus had not yet joined them. 18A strong wind was blowing and the waters grew rough. 19When they had rowed three or three and a half miles, *a* they saw Jesus approaching the boat, walking on the water; and they were terrified. 20But he said to them, "It is I; don't be afraid." 21Then they were willing to take him into the boat, and immediately the boat reached the shore where they were heading.

22The next day the crowd that had stayed on the opposite shore of the lake realized that only one boat had been there, and that Jesus had not entered it with his disciples, but that they had gone away alone. 23Then some boats from Tiberias landed near the place where the people had eaten the bread after the Lord had given thanks. 24Once the crowd realized that neither Jesus nor his disciples were there, they got into the boats and went to Capernaum in search of Jesus.

Jesus the Bread of Life

25When they found him on the other side of the lake, they asked him, "Rabbi, when did you get here?"

26Jesus answered, "I tell you the truth, you are looking for me, not because you saw miraculous signs but because you ate the loaves and had your fill. 27Do not work for food that spoils, but for food that endures to eternal life, which the Son of Man will give you. On him God the Father has placed his seal of approval."

28Then they asked him, "What must we do to do the works God requires?"

29Jesus answered, "The work of God is this: to believe in the one he has sent."

30So they asked him, "What miraculous sign then will you give that we may see it and believe you? What will you do? 31Our forefathers ate the manna in the desert; as it is written: 'He gave them bread from heaven to eat.' *b*"

32Jesus said to them, "I tell you the truth, it is not Moses who has given you the bread from heaven, but it is my Father who gives you the true bread from heaven. 33For the bread of God is he who comes down from heaven and gives life to the world."

34"Sir," they said, "from now on give us this bread."

35Then Jesus declared, "I am the bread of life. He who comes to me will never go hungry, and he who believes in me will never be thirsty. 36But as I told you, you have seen me and still you do not believe. 37All that the Father gives me will come

a19 Greek rowed twenty-five or thirty stadia (about 5 or 6 kilometers)   b31 Exodus 16:4; Neh. 9:15; Psalm 78:24,25

6:16
Mt 14:23-27
Mk 6:47-51

6:27
Isa 55:2
Mt 3:17; 17:5
Mk 1:11; 9:7
Lk 3:22
Jn 1:33; 5:37
8:18
Acts 2:22
Rom 6:23
2 Pet 1:17,18

6:29
1 Thess 1:3
1 Jn 3:23

6:31
Ex 16:4,15
Num 11:7
Ps 78:24; 105:40

6:33
Jn 6:41,50

6:35
Jn 4:14; 6:48
7:37,38

6:37
Jn 10:28,29
17:2,24

6:18 The Sea of Galilee is 650 feet below sea level, 150 feet deep, and surrounded by hills. These physical features make it subject to sudden windstorms causing extremely high waves. Such storms were expected on this sea, but they were nevertheless frightening. When Jesus came to the disciples during a storm, walking on the water (three and a half miles from shore), he told them not to be afraid. We often face spiritual and emotional storms and feel tossed about like a small boat on a big lake. In spite of terrifying circumstances, if we trust our lives to Christ for his safekeeping, he can give us peace in the midst of any storm.

6:18, 19 The disciples, terrified, thought they were seeing a ghost (Mark 6:49). But if they had thought about all they had already seen Jesus do, they could have accepted this miracle. They were frightened—they didn't expect Jesus to come, and they weren't prepared for his help. Faith is a mind-set that *expects* God to act. When we act upon this expectation, we can overcome our fears.

●**6:26** Jesus criticized the people who followed him only for the physical and temporal benefits, not because they were spiritually hungry. Many people use religion to gain prestige, comfort, or even votes. But those are self-centered motives. True believers follow Jesus simply because they know his way is the way to live.

●**6:28, 29** Many sincere seekers for God are puzzled about what he wants them to do. The religions of the world are mankind's attempts to answer this question. But Jesus' reply is brief and simple: we must believe in the one God has sent. Satisfying God does not come from the work we *do,* but from whom we *believe.* The first step is accepting that Jesus is who he claims to be. All spiritual development is built on this affirmation. Declare in prayer to Jesus, "You are the Christ, the Son of the living God," and embark on a life of belief that is satisfying to your Creator.

6:35 People eat bread to satisfy physical hunger and to sustain physical life. We can satisfy spiritual hunger and sustain spiritual life only by a right relationship with Jesus Christ. No wonder he called himself the bread of life. But bread must be eaten to give life, and Christ must be invited into our daily walk to give spiritual life.

6:37, 38 Jesus did not work independently of God the Father, but in union with him. This gives us even more assurance of being welcomed into his presence and being protected by him. Jesus' pur-

6:38
Jn 4:34; 5:30

6:39
Jn 5:24; 10:28
17:12; 18:9

6:40
Jn 1:14,18; 3:16

6:41
Jn 6:33,51,58

6:42
Jn 7:27

6:44
Jn 6:65; 12:32

6:45
Isa 54:13
Jer 31:34
Heb 8:10,11

6:46
Mt 11:27
Lk 10:22
Jn 1:18; 5:37

6:47
Jn 3:16

6:48
Jn 6:58

6:51
Jn 10:10,11

6:54
Jn 6:39

6:56
Jn 15:4; 14:20
17:21-23
Rom 8:9,10

6:57
Jn 5:26; 14:19
15:5
2 Pet 1:3,4

6:58
Jn 6:31

to me, and whoever comes to me I will never drive away. 38For I have come down from heaven not to do my will but to do the will of him who sent me. 39And this is the will of him who sent me, that I shall lose none of all that he has given me, but raise them up at the last day. 40For my Father's will is that everyone who looks to the Son and believes in him shall have eternal life, and I will raise him up at the last day."

41At this the Jews began to grumble about him because he said, "I am the bread that came down from heaven." 42They said, "Is this not Jesus, the son of Joseph, whose father and mother we know? How can he now say, 'I came down from heaven'?"

43"Stop grumbling among yourselves," Jesus answered. 44"No one can come to me unless the Father who sent me draws him, and I will raise him up at the last day. 45It is written in the Prophets: 'They will all be taught by God.'ᵃ Everyone who listens to the Father and learns from him comes to me. 46No one has seen the Father except the one who is from God; only he has seen the Father. 47I tell you the truth, he who believes has everlasting life. 48I am the bread of life. 49Your forefathers ate the manna in the desert, yet they died. 50But here is the bread that comes down from heaven, which a man may eat and not die. 51I am the living bread that came down from heaven. If anyone eats of this bread, he will live forever. This bread is my flesh, which I will give for the life of the world."

52Then the Jews began to argue sharply among themselves, "How can this man give us his flesh to eat?"

53Jesus said to them, "I tell you the truth, unless you eat the flesh of the Son of Man and drink his blood, you have no life in you. 54Whoever eats my flesh and drinks my blood has eternal life, and I will raise him up at the last day. 55For my flesh is real food and my blood is real drink. 56Whoever eats my flesh and drinks my blood remains in me, and I in him. 57Just as the living Father sent me and I live because of the Father, so the one who feeds on me will live because of me. 58This is the bread that came down from heaven. Your forefathers ate manna and died, but

ᵃ45 Isaiah 54:13

pose was to do the will of God, not to satisfy his human desires. When we follow Jesus, we should have the same purpose.

6:39 Jesus said he would not lose even one person that the Father had given him. Thus anyone who makes a sincere commitment to believe in Jesus Christ as Savior is secure in God's promise of eternal life. Christ will not let his people be overcome by Satan and lose their salvation (see also 17:12; Philippians 1:6).

6:40 Those who put their faith in Jesus will be resurrected from physical death to eternal life with God when Christ comes again (see 1 Corinthians 15:52; 1 Thessalonians 4:16).

6:41 When John says *Jews,* he is referring to the Jewish leaders who were hostile to Jesus, not to Jews in general. John himself was a Jew, and so was Jesus.

●**6:41** The religious leaders grumbled because they could not accept Jesus' claim of divinity. They saw him only as a carpenter from Nazareth. They refused to believe he was God's divine Son, and they could not tolerate his message. Many people reject Christ because they say they cannot believe he is the Son of God. In reality, the claims he makes for their loyalty and obedience are what they can't accept; they don't want to change. So to protect themselves from God's message, they deny the messenger.

6:44 God, not man, plays the most active role in salvation. When someone chooses to believe in Jesus Christ as Savior, he does so only in response to the urging of God's Holy Spirit. God does the urging; then we decide whether or not to believe. Thus no one can believe in Jesus without God's help.

6:45 Jesus is alluding to an Old Testament view of the messianic kingdom in which all people are taught directly by God (Isaiah 54:13; Jeremiah 31:31-34). He is stressing the importance of not

merely hearing, but learning. We are taught by God through the Bible, our experiences, the thoughts the Holy Spirit brings, and other Christians. Are you open to his teaching?

6:47 *Believes* as used here means "continues to believe." We do not believe merely once; we keep on believing or trusting Jesus.

6:47ff The religious leaders frequently asked Jesus to prove to them why he was better than the prophets they already had. Jesus here refers to the manna that Moses gave their ancestors in the desert (see Exodus 16). This bread was physical and temporal. The people ate it, and it sustained them for a day; but they had to get more bread every day, and this bread could not keep them from dying. Jesus, who is much greater than Moses, offers himself as the spiritual bread from heaven that satisfies completely and leads to eternal life. Are you trusting him to sustain you?

6:51 How can Jesus give us his flesh as bread to eat? To eat living bread means to unite ourselves to Christ. We are united with Christ in two ways: (1) by believing in his death (the sacrifice of his flesh) and resurrection and (2) by devoting ourselves to living as he requires, depending on his teaching for guidance and trusting in the Holy Spirit for power.

6:56 This was a shocking message—to eat flesh and drink blood sounded cannibalistic. The idea of drinking any blood, let alone human blood, was repugnant to the religious leaders because the law forbade it (Leviticus 17:10, 11). Jesus was not talking about literal blood, of course. He was saying that his life had to become their own, but they could not accept this concept. The apostle Paul later used the body and blood imagery in talking about the Lord's Supper (see 1 Corinthians 11:23–26).

he who feeds on this bread will live forever." 59He said this while teaching in the synagogue in Capernaum.

6:59
Mt 4:23

Many Disciples Desert Jesus

60On hearing it, many of his disciples said, "This is a hard teaching. Who can accept it?"

6:62
Mk 16:19
Jn 3:13

61Aware that his disciples were grumbling about this, Jesus said to them, "Does this offend you? 62What if you see the Son of Man ascend to where he was before! 63The Spirit gives life; the flesh counts for nothing. The words I have spoken to you are spirit*a* and they are life. 64Yet there are some of you who do not believe." For Jesus had known from the beginning which of them did not believe and who would betray him. 65He went on to say, "This is why I told you that no one can come to me unless the Father has enabled him."

6:63
Jn 3:34
Rom 8:2

6:64
Mt 10:4
Jn 13:11

6:65
Jn 6:37,44

6:66
Lk 9:62
Heb 10:38
1 Jn 2:19

66From this time many of his disciples turned back and no longer followed him.

67"You do not want to leave too, do you?" Jesus asked the Twelve.

68Simon Peter answered him, "Lord, to whom shall we go? You have the words of eternal life. 69We believe and know that you are the Holy One of God."

6:68
Jn 3:34; 5:25,26

6:69
Acts 3:14
1 Jn 2:20

70Then Jesus replied, "Have I not chosen you, the Twelve? Yet one of you is a devil!" 71(He meant Judas, the son of Simon Iscariot, who, though one of the Twelve, was later to betray him.)

6:70
Mt 10:2-4
Jn 13:2,27

2. Jesus Encounters Conflict With the Religious Leaders
Jesus Goes to the Feast of Tabernacles

7 After this, Jesus went around in Galilee, purposely staying away from Judea because the Jews there were waiting to take his life. 2But when the Jewish Feast of Tabernacles was near, 3Jesus' brothers said to him, "You ought to leave here and go to Judea, so that your disciples may see the miracles you do. 4No one who wants to become a public figure acts in secret. Since you are doing these things, show yourself to the world." 5For even his own brothers did not believe in him.

7:1
Jn 5:18; 7:19
8:37

7:2
Lev 23:23,24

7:3
Mt 12:46
Mk 3:31,32
Acts 1:14

6Therefore Jesus told them, "The right time for me has not yet come; for you any time is right. 7The world cannot hate you, but it hates me because I testify that what it does is evil. 8 You go to the Feast. I am not yet*b* going up to this Feast, because

7:6
Jn 2:4

7:7
Jn 3:19
15:18,19

a63 Or *Spirit*   *b 8* Some early manuscripts do not have *yet.*

6:63, 65 The Holy Spirit gives spiritual life; without the work of the Holy Spirit we cannot even see our need for it (14:17). All spiritual renewal begins and ends with God. He reveals truth to us, lives within us, then he enables us to respond to that truth.

●**6:66** Why did Jesus' words cause many of his followers to desert him? (1) They may have realized that he wasn't one to be the conquering Messiah-king they expected. (2) He refused to give in to their self-centered requests. (3) He emphasized faith, not works. (4) His teachings were difficult to understand, and some of his words were offensive. As we grow in our faith, we may be tempted to turn away because Jesus' lessons are hard. Will your response be to give up, ignore certain teachings, or reject Christ? Instead, ask God to show you what the teachings mean and how they apply to your life. Then have the courage to act upon God's truth.

6:67 There is no middle ground with Jesus. When he asked the disciples if they would also leave, he was showing that they could either accept or reject him. Jesus was not trying to repel people with his teachings. He was simply telling the truth. The more the people heard Jesus' real message, the more they divided into two camps—the honest seekers who wanted to understand more and those who rejected Jesus because they didn't like what they heard.

●**6:67, 68** After many of Jesus' followers had deserted him, he asked the 12 disciples if they were also going to leave. Peter responded, "To whom shall we go?" In his straightforward way, Peter answered for all of us—there is no other way. Though there are many philosophies and self-styled authorities, Jesus alone has the

words that give eternal life. People look everywhere for eternal life and miss Christ, the only source. Stay with him, especially when you are confused or feel alone.

●**6:70** In response to Jesus' message, some people left; others stayed and truly believed; and some, like Judas, stayed but tried to use Jesus for personal gain. Many today turn away from Christ. Others pretend to follow, going to church for status, approval of family and friends, or business contacts. But there are only two real responses to Jesus—you either accept or reject him. How have you responded to Christ?

6:71 For more information on Judas, see his Profile in Mark 14.

7:2 The Feast of Tabernacles is described in Leviticus 23:33ff. This event occurred in October, about six months after the Passover celebration mentioned in John 6:2–5. The feast commemorated the days when the Israelites wandered in the desert and lived in tents (Leviticus 23:43).

●**7:3-5** Jesus' brothers had a difficult time believing in him. Some of these brothers would eventually become leaders in the church, but for several years they were embarrassed by him. After Jesus died and rose again, they finally believed. We today have every reason to believe because we have the full record of Jesus' miracles, death, and resurrection. We also have the evidence of what the gospel has done in people's lives through the centuries. Don't miss this opportunity to believe in God's Son.

7:7 Because the world hated Jesus, we who follow him can expect that many people will hate us as well. If circumstances are going

for me the right time has not yet come." 9Having said this, he stayed in Galilee.

7:11
Jn 11:56

10However, after his brothers had left for the Feast, he went also, not publicly, but in secret. 11Now at the Feast the Jews were watching for him and asking, "Where is that man?"

7:12
Mt 21:45,46
Lk 7:16
Jn 7:40-43
9:16; 10:19

12Among the crowds there was widespread whispering about him. Some said, "He is a good man."

7:13
Jn 9:22,23

Others replied, "No, he deceives the people." 13But no one would say anything publicly about him for fear of the Jews.

Jesus Teaches at the Feast

14Not until halfway through the Feast did Jesus go up to the temple courts and begin to teach. 15The Jews were amazed and asked, "How did this man get such learning without having studied?"

7:15
Acts 4:13; 22:3
2 Tim 3:15

7:16
Jn 8:28; 12:49

16Jesus answered, "My teaching is not my own. It comes from him who sent me. 17If anyone chooses to do God's will, he will find out whether my teaching comes from God or whether I speak on my own. 18He who speaks on his own does so to gain honor for himself, but he who works for the honor of the one who sent him is a man of truth; there is nothing false about him. 19Has not Moses given you the law? Yet not one of you keeps the law. Why are you trying to kill me?"

7:17
Hos 6:1-3

7:18
Jn 5:41; 8:50,54

7:19
Jn 1:17; 7:1

7:20
Jn 8:48-52
10:20

20"You are demon-possessed," the crowd answered. "Who is trying to kill you?"

21Jesus said to them, "I did one miracle, and you are all astonished. 22Yet, because Moses gave you circumcision (though actually it did not come from Moses, but from the patriarchs), you circumcise a child on the Sabbath. 23Now if a child can be circumcised on the Sabbath so that the law of Moses may not be broken, why are you angry with me for healing the whole man on the Sabbath? 24Stop judging by mere appearances, and make a right judgment."

7:21,22
Gen 17:9,10
Lev 12:3
Jn 5:8
Acts 7:8

7:23
Jn 5:10

Is Jesus the Christ?

25At that point some of the people of Jerusalem began to ask, "Isn't this the man they are trying to kill? 26Here he is, speaking publicly, and they are not saying a word to him. Have the authorities really concluded that he is the Christ*a*? 27 But we

7:27
Jn 7:41,42
9:29

a 26 Or Messiah; also in verses 27, 31, 41 and 42

---

too well, ask if you are following him as you should. We can be grateful if life goes well, but not at the cost of following Jesus half-heartedly or not at all.

7:10 Jesus came with the greatest gift ever offered, so why did he often act secretly? The religious leaders hated him and refused his gift of salvation. The more he taught and worked publicly, the more these leaders caused trouble for Jesus and his followers. So it was necessary for Jesus to teach and work as quietly as possible. Many people today have the privilege of teaching, preaching, and worshiping publicly with little persecution. These believers should thankfully take advantage of their freedom.

●**7:13** The religious leaders had a great deal of power over the common people. It is apparent that they couldn't do much to Jesus at this time, but they threatened anyone who might publicly support him. Excommunication from the synagogue was one of the reprisals (9:22). To a Jew, this was a severe punishment.

●**7:13** Everyone was talking about Jesus! But when it came time to speak up for him in public, no one said a word. All were afraid. Fear can stifle our witness. Although many people talk about Christ in church, when it comes to making a public statement about their faith, they are often embarrassed. Jesus says that he will acknowledge us before God if we acknowledge him before others (Matthew 10:32). Be courageous! Speak up for Christ!

7:16–18 Those who seek and do God's will know Jesus was telling the truth about himself. Have you ever listened to religious speakers and wondered if they were telling the truth? Test them: (1) ask if their words agree with or contradict the Bible, and (2) ask if their words point to God and doing his will or to themselves.

●**7:19** The Pharisees spent their days trying to achieve holiness by keeping the meticulous rules they had added to God's laws. Jesus' accusation that they didn't keep Moses' laws stung them deeply. In spite of their pompous pride in themselves and their rules, they did not even fulfill a legalistic religion, for they were living far below what the Law of Moses required. Jesus' followers should do *more* than the moral law requires, not by adding to its requirements, but by going beyond the do's and don'ts to the spirit of the law.

7:20 Most of the people were probably not aware of the plot to kill Jesus (5:18). There was a small group looking for the right opportunity to kill him, but most were still trying to decide what they believed about him.

7:21–23 According to Moses' Law, circumcision was to be performed eight days after a baby's birth (Genesis 17:9–14; Leviticus 12:3). If it was a Sabbath, the circumcision was still performed (even though it was considered work). While the religious leaders allowed certain exceptions to Sabbath laws, they allowed none to Jesus, who was simply showing mercy to those who needed healing.

●**7:26** This chapter shows the many reactions people had toward Jesus. They called him a good man (7:12), a deceiver (7:12), a demon-possessed man (7:20), the Christ (7:26), and the Prophet (7:40). We must make up our own minds about who Jesus is, knowing that whatever we decide will have eternal consequences.

7:27 Popular tradition said the Messiah would simply appear. But Scripture actually predicted his birthplace (Micah 5:2).

know where this man is from; when the Christ comes, no one will know where he is from."

²⁸Then Jesus, still teaching in the temple courts, cried out, "Yes, you know me, and you know where I am from. I am not here on my own, but he who sent me is true. You do not know him, ²⁹but I know him because I am from him and he sent me."

³⁰At this they tried to seize him, but no one laid a hand on him, because his time had not yet come. ³¹Still, many in the crowd put their faith in him. They said, "When the Christ comes, will he do more miraculous signs than this man?"

³²The Pharisees heard the crowd whispering such things about him. Then the chief priests and the Pharisees sent temple guards to arrest him.

³³Jesus said, "I am with you for only a short time, and then I go to the one who sent me. ³⁴You will look for me, but you will not find me; and where I am, you cannot come."

³⁵The Jews said to one another, "Where does this man intend to go that we cannot find him? Will he go where our people live scattered among the Greeks, and teach the Greeks? ³⁶What did he mean when he said, 'You will look for me, but you will not find me,' and 'Where I am, you cannot come'?"

³⁷On the last and greatest day of the Feast, Jesus stood and said in a loud voice, "If anyone is thirsty, let him come to me and drink. ³⁸Whoever believes in me, as ᵃ the Scripture has said, streams of living water will flow from within him." ³⁹By this he meant the Spirit, whom those who believed in him were later to receive. Up to that time the Spirit had not been given, since Jesus had not yet been glorified.

⁴⁰On hearing his words, some of the people said, "Surely this man is the Prophet."

⁴¹Others said, "He is the Christ."

Still others asked, "How can the Christ come from Galilee? ⁴²Does not the Scripture say that the Christ will come from David's family ᵇ and from Bethlehem, the town where David lived?" ⁴³Thus the people were divided because of Jesus. ⁴⁴Some wanted to seize him, but no one laid a hand on him.

Unbelief of the Jewish Leaders

⁴⁵Finally the temple guards went back to the chief priests and Pharisees, who asked them, "Why didn't you bring him in?"

⁴⁶"No one ever spoke the way this man does," the guards declared.

⁴⁷"You mean he has deceived you also?" the Pharisees retorted. ⁴⁸"Has any of the rulers or of the Pharisees believed in him? ⁴⁹No! But this mob that knows nothing of the law—there is a curse on them."

⁵⁰Nicodemus, who had gone to Jesus earlier and who was one of their own num-

ᵃ37,38 Or / If anyone is thirsty, let him come to me. / And let him drink, ³⁸who believes in me. / As   ᵇ42 Greek seed

7:28 Jn 1:18; 5:43 8:14,26,55
7:29 Mt 11:27 Jn 3:17; 8:55 10:15; 17:25
7:33 Jn 14:19 16:5,10,16-18
7:34 Jn 8:21; 13:33
7:37 Isa 55:1 Jn 4:10,14 6:35 Rev 22:17
7:38 Isa 12:3; 44:3 58:11 Ezek 47:1-10 Joel 3:18
7:39 Jn 14:17,18; 16:7 20:22 Rom 8:9 1 Cor 15:45 2 Cor 3:17
7:40 Deut 18:15 Jn 1:21; 6:14
7:41,42 1 Sam 16:1 2 Sam 7:12 Ps 132:11 Mic 5:2
7:43 Jn 9:16; 10:19
7:46 Lk 4:22
7:48 1 Cor 1:20
7:50 Jn 3:1,2; 19:39

7:37 Jesus' words "come to me and drink" alluded to the theme of many Bible passages that talk about the Messiah's life-giving blessings (Isaiah 12:2, 3; 44:3, 4; 58:11). In promising to give the Holy Spirit to all who believed, Jesus was claiming to be the Messiah, for that was something only the Messiah could do.

7:38 Jesus used the term *living water* in 4:10 to indicate eternal life. Here he uses the term to refer to the Holy Spirit. The two go together: wherever the Holy Spirit is accepted, he brings eternal life. Jesus teaches more about the Holy Spirit in chapters 14—16. The Holy Spirit empowered Jesus' followers at Pentecost (Acts 2) and has since been available to all who believe in Jesus as Savior.

7:40-43 The crowd was asking questions about Jesus. Some believed, others were hostile, and others disqualified Jesus as the Messiah because he was from Nazareth, not Bethlehem (Micah 5:2). But he *was* born in Bethlehem (Luke 2:1–7), although he grew up in Nazareth. If they had looked more carefully, they would not have jumped to the wrong conclusions. When you search for God's truth, make sure you look carefully and thoughtfully at the Bible with an open heart and mind. Don't jump to conclusions before knowing more of what the Bible says.

7:44–46 Although the Romans ruled Palestine, they gave the Jewish religious leaders authority over minor civil and religious affairs. The religious leaders controlled their own temple guard and gave the officers power to arrest anyone causing a disturbance or breaking any of their ceremonial laws. Because these leaders had developed hundreds of trivial laws, it was almost impossible for anyone, even the leaders themselves, not to break, neglect, or ignore at least a few of them some of the time. But these officers couldn't find one reason to arrest Jesus. And as they listened to him to try to find evidence, they couldn't help hearing the wonderful words he said.

● **7:46–49** The Jewish leaders saw themselves as an elite group who alone had the truth, and they resisted the truth about Christ because it wasn't *theirs* to begin with. It is easy to think that we have the truth and that those who disagree with us do not have any truth at all. But God's truth is available to everyone. Don't repeat the Pharisees' self-centered and narrow attitude.

7:51
Ex 23:1
Deut 17:2-8
19:15-19
Prov 18:13

7:52
Isa 9:1,2
Mt 4:14-16
Jn 1:46

ber, asked, ⁵¹"Does our law condemn anyone without first hearing him to find out what he is doing?"

⁵²They replied, "Are you from Galilee, too? Look into it, and you will find that a prophet*a* does not come out of Galilee."

[The earliest manuscripts and many other ancient witnesses do not have John 7:53–8:11.]

⁵³Then each went to his own home.

8 But Jesus went to the Mount of Olives. ²At dawn he appeared again in the temple courts, where all the people gathered around him, and he sat down to teach them. ³The teachers of the law and the Pharisees brought in a woman caught in adultery. They made her stand before the group ⁴and said to Jesus, "Teacher, this woman was caught in the act of adultery. ⁵In the Law Moses commanded us to stone such women. Now what do you say?" ⁶They were using this question as a trap, in order to have a basis for accusing him.

8:5
Ex 20:14
Lev 18:20; 20:10
Deut 5:18; 22:22
Job 31:9-11
Mt 5:27,28

8:7
Deut 17:7

But Jesus bent down and started to write on the ground with his finger. ⁷When they kept on questioning him, he straightened up and said to them, "If any one of you is without sin, let him be the first to throw a stone at her." ⁸Again he stooped down and wrote on the ground.

⁹At this, those who heard began to go away one at a time, the older ones first, until only Jesus was left, with the woman still standing there. ¹⁰Jesus straightened up and asked her, "Woman, where are they? Has no one condemned you?"

8:11
Jn 5:14

¹¹"No one, sir," she said.

"Then neither do I condemn you," Jesus declared. "Go now and leave your life of sin."

a52 Two early manuscripts *the Prophet*

● **7:50–52** This passage offers additional insight into Nicodemus, the Pharisee who visited Jesus at night (chapter 3). Apparently Nicodemus had become a secret believer. Since most of the Pharisees hated Jesus and wanted to kill him, Nicodemus risked his reputation and high position when he spoke up for Jesus. His statement was bold, and the Pharisees immediately became suspicious. After Jesus' death, Nicodemus brought spices for his body (19:39). That is the last time he is mentioned in Scripture.

● **7:51** Nicodemus confronted the Pharisees with their failure to keep their own laws. The Pharisees were losing ground—the temple guards came back impressed by Jesus (7:46), and one of their own, Nicodemus, was defending him. With their hypocritical motives exposed and their prestige eroding, they began to protect themselves. Pride interfered with their ability to reason, and soon they became obsessed with getting rid of Jesus just to save face. What was good and right no longer mattered.

8:3–6 The Jewish leaders had already disregarded the law by arresting the woman without the man. The law required that both parties to adultery be stoned (Leviticus 20:10; Deuteronomy 22:22). The leaders were using the woman as a trap so they could trick Jesus. If Jesus said the woman should not be stoned, they would accuse him of violating Moses' Law. If he urged them to execute her, they would report him to the Romans, who did not permit the Jews to carry out their own executions.

8:7 This is a significant statement about judging others. Because he upheld the legal penalty for adultery, stoning, Jesus could not be accused of being against the law. But by saying that only a sinless person could throw the first stone, he highlighted the impor-

tance of compassion and forgiveness. When others are caught in sin, are you quick to pass judgment? To do so is to act as though you have never sinned. It is God's role to judge, not ours. Our role is to show forgiveness and compassion.

8:8 It is uncertain whether Jesus was merely ignoring them by writing on the ground, writing out the Ten Commandments, or listing the sins of the participants.

8:9 When Jesus said that only someone who had not sinned should throw the first stone, the leaders slipped quietly away, from eldest to youngest. Evidently the older men were more aware of their sins than the younger. Age and experience often temper youthful self-righteousness. But whatever your age, take an honest look at your life. Recognize your sinful nature, and look for ways to help others rather than hurt them.

8:11 Jesus didn't condemn the woman accused of adultery, but neither did he ignore or condone her sin. He told her to go and sin no more. Jesus stands ready to forgive any sin in your life, but confession and repentance mean a change of heart. With God's help we can accept Christ's forgiveness and stop our wrongdoing.

The Validity of Jesus' Testimony

¹²When Jesus spoke again to the people, he said, "I am the light of the world. Whoever follows me will never walk in darkness, but will have the light of life."

¹³The Pharisees challenged him, "Here you are, appearing as your own witness; your testimony is not valid."

¹⁴Jesus answered, "Even if I testify on my own behalf, my testimony is valid, for I know where I came from and where I am going. But you have no idea where I come from or where I am going. ¹⁵You judge by human standards; I pass judgment on no one. ¹⁶But if I do judge, my decisions are right, because I am not alone. I stand with the Father, who sent me. ¹⁷In your own Law it is written that the testimony of two men is valid. ¹⁸I am one who testifies for myself; my other witness is the Father, who sent me."

¹⁹Then they asked him, "Where is your father?"

"You do not know me or my Father," Jesus replied. "If you knew me, you would know my Father also." ²⁰He spoke these words while teaching in the temple area near the place where the offerings were put. Yet no one seized him, because his time had not yet come.

²¹Once more Jesus said to them, "I am going away, and you will look for me, and you will die in your sin. Where I go, you cannot come."

²²This made the Jews ask, "Will he kill himself? Is that why he says, 'Where I go, you cannot come'?"

²³But he continued, "You are from below; I am from above. You are of this world; I am not of this world. ²⁴I told you that you would die in your sins; if you do not believe that I am ⌊the one I claim to be⌋,ᵃ you will indeed die in your sins."

²⁵"Who are you?" they asked.

"Just what I have been claiming all along," Jesus replied. ²⁶"I have much to say in judgment of you. But he who sent me is reliable, and what I have heard from him I tell the world."

²⁷They did not understand that he was telling them about his Father. ²⁸So Jesus said, "When you have lifted up the Son of Man, then you will know that I am ⌊the one I claim to be⌋ and that I do nothing on my own but speak just what the Father has taught me. ²⁹The one who sent me is with me; he has not left me alone, for I always do what pleases him." ³⁰Even as he spoke, many put their faith in him.

The Children of Abraham

³¹To the Jews who had believed him, Jesus said, "If you hold to my teaching, you are really my disciples. ³²Then you will know the truth, and the truth will set you free."

ᵃ24 Or I am he; also in verse 28

8:12
Isa 9:1,2
Jn 1:4,5,9; 3:19
9:5; 12:35,36,46
2 Cor 4:6

8:14
Jn 7:28; 18:37
Rev 1:5

8:16
Jn 5:30
14:10,11; 16:32

8:17
Deut 17:6; 19:15

8:18
Jn 5:37

8:19
Jn 14:7,9

8:20
Mk 12:41
Lk 21:1
Jn 7:30

8:21
Jn 7:34; 13:33

8:22
Jn 7:35,36

8:23
Jn 3:31; 15:19
17:16
1 Jn 4:5

8:24
Ex 3:14,15
Jn 4:26; 8:28,58

8:26
Jn 3:32-34
12:49; 15:15

8:28
Jn 3:11,14,15
5:19; 8:24; 12:32
Rom 1:4

8:29
Jn 4:34; 6:38
14:10; 16:32

8:31
Jn 15:7

8:32
Gal 5:1,13

8:12 To understand what Jesus meant by *the light of the world*, see the notes on 1:4 and 1:4, 5.

8:12 Jesus was speaking in the part of the temple known as the treasury (8:20) where candles burned to symbolize the pillar of fire that led the people of Israel through the desert (Exodus 13:21, 22). In this context, Jesus called himself the light of the world. The pillar of fire represented God's presence, protection, and guidance. Jesus brings God's presence, protection, and guidance. Is he the light of *your* world?

8:12 What does it mean to follow Christ? As a soldier follows his captain, so we should follow Christ, our commander. As a slave follows his master, so we should follow Christ, our Lord. As we follow the advice of a trusted counselor, so we should follow Jesus' commands to us in Scripture. As we follow the laws of our nation, so we should follow the laws of the kingdom of heaven.

8:13, 14 The Pharisees thought Jesus was either insane or a liar. Jesus provided them with a third alternative: he was telling the truth. Because most of the Pharisees refused to consider the third alternative, they never recognized him as Messiah and Lord. If you

are seeking to know who Jesus is, do not close any door before looking through it honestly. Only with an open mind will you know the truth that he is Messiah and Lord.

8:13–18 The Pharisees argued that Jesus' claim was legally invalid because he had no other witnesses. Jesus responded that his confirming witness was God himself. He and God made two witnesses, the number required by the law (Deuteronomy 19:15).

8:20 The temple treasury was located in the court of women. In this area, 13 collection boxes were set up to receive money offerings. Seven of the boxes were for the temple tax; the other six were for freewill offerings. On another occasion, a widow placed her money in one of these boxes and Jesus taught a profound lesson from her action (Luke 21:1–4).

8:24 People will die in their sins if they reject Christ, because they are rejecting the only way to be rescued from sin. Sadly, many are so taken up with the values of this world that they are blind to the priceless gift Christ offers. Where are you looking? Don't focus on this world's values and miss what is most valuable—eternal life with God.

8:32 Jesus himself is the truth that makes us free (8:36). He is the

8:33
Lev 25:42
Mt 3:9

8:34
Rom 6:16
2 Pet 2:19

8:35
Gen 21:10
Gal 4:30

8:39
Mt 3:9
Rom 3:28; 9:7
Gal 3:7,29

8:41
Deut 32:6
Isa 63:16; 64:8
Mal 1:6

8:42
Jn 1:14; 3:16
5:43; 16:27

8:44
1 Jn 2:4; 3:8

8:45
Jn 18:37

8:47
1 Jn 4:6

8:49
Jn 7:20

8:50
Jn 5:41,42

8:51
Jn 5:24
11:25,26

33They answered him, "We are Abraham's descendants*a* and have never been slaves of anyone. How can you say that we shall be set free?"

34Jesus replied, "I tell you the truth, everyone who sins is a slave to sin. 35Now a slave has no permanent place in the family, but a son belongs to it forever. 36So if the Son sets you free, you will be free indeed. 37I know you are Abraham's descendants. Yet you are ready to kill me, because you have no room for my word. 38I am telling you what I have seen in the Father's presence, and you do what you have heard from your father.*b*"

39"Abraham is our father," they answered.

"If you were Abraham's children," said Jesus, "then you would*c* do the things Abraham did. 40As it is, you are determined to kill me, a man who has told you the truth that I heard from God. Abraham did not do such things. 41You are doing the things your own father does."

"We are not illegitimate children," they protested. "The only Father we have is God himself."

The Children of the Devil

42Jesus said to them, "If God were your Father, you would love me, for I came from God and now am here. I have not come on my own; but he sent me. 43Why is my language not clear to you? Because you are unable to hear what I say. 44You belong to your father, the devil, and you want to carry out your father's desire. He was a murderer from the beginning, not holding to the truth, for there is no truth in him. When he lies, he speaks his native language, for he is a liar and the father of lies. 45Yet because I tell the truth, you do not believe me! 46Can any of you prove me guilty of sin? If I am telling the truth, why don't you believe me? 47He who belongs to God hears what God says. The reason you do not hear is that you do not belong to God."

The Claims of Jesus About Himself

48The Jews answered him, "Aren't we right in saying that you are a Samaritan and demon-possessed?"

49"I am not possessed by a demon," said Jesus, "but I honor my Father and you dishonor me. 50I am not seeking glory for myself; but there is one who seeks it, and he is the judge. 51I tell you the truth, if anyone keeps my word, he will never see death."

a33 Greek seed; also in verse 37   b38 Or presence. Therefore do what you have heard from the Father.
c39 Some early manuscripts "If you are Abraham's children," said Jesus, "then

---

source of truth, the perfect standard of what is right. He frees us from the consequences of sin, from self-deception, and from deception by Satan. He shows us clearly the way to eternal life with God. Thus Jesus does not give us freedom to do what we want, but freedom to follow God. As we seek to serve God, Jesus' perfect truth frees us to be all that God meant us to be.

●**8:34, 35** Sin has a way of enslaving us, controlling us, dominating us, and dictating our actions. Jesus can free you from this slavery that keeps you from becoming the person God created you to be. If sin is restraining, mastering, or enslaving you, Jesus can break its power over your life.

8:41 Jesus made a distinction between hereditary children and *true* children. The religious leaders were hereditary children of Abraham (founder of the Jewish nation) and therefore claimed to be children of God. But their actions showed them to be true children of Satan, for they lived under Satan's guidance. True children of Abraham (faithful followers of God) would not act as they did. Your church membership and family connections will not make you true children of God. Your true father is the one you obey.

8:43 The religious leaders were prevented from understanding because they refused to listen. Satan used their stubbornness, pride, and prejudices to keep them from believing in Jesus.

8:44, 45 The attitudes and actions of these leaders clearly identi-

fied them as followers of Satan. They may not have been conscious of this, but their hatred of truth, their lies, and their murderous intentions indicated how much control Satan had over them. They were his tools in carrying out his plans; they spoke the same language of lies. Satan still uses people to obstruct God's work (Genesis 4:8; Romans 5:12; 1 John 3:12).

8:46 No one could accuse Jesus of a single sin. People who hated him and wanted him dead scrutinized his behavior but could find nothing wrong. Jesus proved he was God in the flesh by his sinless life. He is the only perfect example for us to follow.

8:46, 47 In a number of places Jesus intentionally challenged his listeners to test him. He welcomed those who were willing to question through on what they discovered. His challenge clarifies the two most frequent reasons that people miss encountering him: (1) they never accept his challenge to test him, or (2) they test him but are not willing to believe what they discover. Have you made either of those mistakes?

8:51 To keep Jesus' word means to hear his words and obey them. When Jesus says those who obey won't die, he is talking about spiritual death, not physical death. Even physical death, however, will eventually be overcome. Those who follow Jesus will be raised to live eternally with him.

52At this the Jews exclaimed, "Now we know that you are demon-possessed! Abraham died and so did the prophets, yet you say that if anyone keeps your word, he will never taste death. 53Are you greater than our father Abraham? He died, and so did the prophets. Who do you think you are?"

54Jesus replied, "If I glorify myself, my glory means nothing. My Father, whom you claim as your God, is the one who glorifies me. 55Though you do not know him, I know him. If I said I did not, I would be a liar like you, but I do know him and keep his word. 56Your father Abraham rejoiced at the thought of seeing my day; he saw it and was glad."

57"You are not yet fifty years old," the Jews said to him, "and you have seen Abraham!"

58"I tell you the truth," Jesus answered, "before Abraham was born, I am!" 59At this, they picked up stones to stone him, but Jesus hid himself, slipping away from the temple grounds.

8:53 Jn 4:12
8:54 Jn 16:14; 17:1
8:55 Jn 7:29; 15:10
8:56 Gen 22:17,18
Lk 10:24
Gal 3:8,9,16
Heb 11:10,13
8:58 Ex 3:14
Isa 9:6; 43:13
Mic 5:2
Jn 8:24,28
13:19
Col 1:17
Heb 13:8
Rev 1:8

Jesus Heals a Man Born Blind

9 As he went along, he saw a man blind from birth. 2His disciples asked him, "Rabbi, who sinned, this man or his parents, that he was born blind?"

3"Neither this man nor his parents sinned," said Jesus, "but this happened so that the work of God might be displayed in his life. 4As long as it is day, we must do the work of him who sent me. Night is coming, when no one can work. 5While I am in the world, I am the light of the world."

annointed

6Having said this, he spit on the ground, made some mud with the saliva, and put it on the man's eyes. 7"Go," he told him, "wash in the Pool of Siloam" (this word means Sent). So the man went and washed, and came home seeing.

8His neighbors and those who had formerly seen him begging asked, "Isn't this the same man who used to sit and beg?" 9Some claimed that he was.

Others said, "No, he only looks like him."

But he himself insisted, "I am the man."

10"How then were your eyes opened?" they demanded.

11He replied, "The man they call Jesus made some mud and put it on my eyes. He told me to go to Siloam and wash. So I went and washed, and then I could see."

12"Where is this man?" they asked him.

"I don't know," he said.

9:1 Ex 20:5
9:3 Jn 11:4
9:4 Jn 4:34
5:19,36; 11:9
12:35; 17:4
9:5 Isa 9:2; 42:6
49:6
Lk 2:32
Jn 1:5,9; 3:19
8:12; 12:46
9:6 Mk 7:33; 8:23
9:7 2 Kgs 5:14
Neh 3:15
Isa 35:5
9:8 Acts 3:2,10

The Pharisees Investigate the Healing

13They brought to the Pharisees the man who had been blind. 14Now the day on

---

8:56 God told Abraham, father of the Jewish nation, that through him all nations would be blessed (Genesis 12:1–7; 15:1–21). Abraham had been able to see this through the eyes of faith. Jesus, a descendant of Abraham, blessed all people through his death, resurrection, and offer of salvation.

8:58 This is one of the most powerful statements uttered by Jesus. When he says he existed before Abraham was born, he undeniably proclaims his divinity. Not only did Jesus say he existed before Abraham, he also applied God's holy name (*I Am*—Exodus 3:14) to himself. This claim demands a response. It cannot be ignored. The Jewish leaders tried to stone him for blasphemy because he claimed equality with God. But Jesus is God. How have you responded to Jesus, the Son of God?

8:59 In accordance with the law in Leviticus 24:16, the religious leaders were ready to stone Jesus for claiming to be God. They well understood what Jesus was claiming, and since they didn't believe him, they charged him with blasphemy. How ironic that they were really the blasphemers, cursing and attacking the very God they claimed to serve!

9:1ff In chapter 9, we see four different reactions to Jesus. The neighbors revealed surprise and skepticism; the Pharisees showed disbelief and prejudice; the parents believed but kept quiet for fear

of excommunication; and the healed man showed consistent, growing belief.

●**9:2, 3** A common belief in Jewish culture was that calamity or suffering was the result of some great sin. But Christ used this man's suffering to teach about faith and to glorify God. We live in a fallen world where good behavior is not always rewarded and bad behavior not always punished. Therefore, innocent people sometimes suffer. If God took suffering away whenever we asked, we would follow him for comfort and convenience, not out of love and devotion. Regardless of the reasons for our suffering, Jesus has the power to help us deal with it. When you suffer from a disease, tragedy, or handicap, try not to ask, "Why did this happen to me?" or "What did I do wrong?" Instead, ask God to give you strength for the trial and offer you a clearer perspective on what is happening.

9:7 The pool of Siloam was made by Hezekiah. His workers built an underground tunnel from a spring outside the city walls to carry water into the city. Thus the people could always get water without fear of being attacked. This was especially important in times of siege (see 2 Kings 20:20; 2 Chronicles 32:30).

●**9:13–17** While the Pharisees questioned and debated about Jesus, people were being healed and lives were being changed. Their skepticism was based not on insufficient evidence, but on

9:14
Jn 5:9

9:16
Jn 3:2; 7:12,43

9:17
Deut 18:15
Mt 21:11
Jn 4:19; 6:14

9:22
Jn 7:13; 12:42
16:2; 19:38
Acts 5:13

9:24
Josh 7:19

9:28
Jn 5:45
Rom 2:17
9:29
Jn 1:10; 8:14
9:31
Job 27:8,9
Ps 34:15; 66:18
Isa 1:15
Jer 11:11; 14:12
Mic 3:4
Zech 7:13
9:33
Jn 3:2

9:35
Mt 16:16

9:37
Jn 4:26

which Jesus had made the mud and opened the man's eyes was a Sabbath. 15Therefore the Pharisees also asked him how he had received his sight. "He put mud on my eyes," the man replied, "and I washed, and now I see."

16Some of the Pharisees said, "This man is not from God, for he does not keep the Sabbath."

But others asked, "How can a sinner do such miraculous signs?" So they were divided.

17Finally they turned again to the blind man, "What have you to say about him? It was your eyes he opened."

The man replied, "He is a prophet."

18The Jews still did not believe that he had been blind and had received his sight until they sent for the man's parents. 19"Is this your son?" they asked. "Is this the one you say was born blind? How is it that now he can see?"

20"We know he is our son," the parents answered, "and we know he was born blind. 21But how he can see now, or who opened his eyes, we don't know. Ask him. He is of age; he will speak for himself." 22His parents said this because they were afraid of the Jews, for already the Jews had decided that anyone who acknowledged that Jesus was the Christ*a* would be put out of the synagogue. 23That was why his parents said, "He is of age; ask him."

24A second time they summoned the man who had been blind. "Give glory to God,*b*" they said. "We know this man is a sinner."

25He replied, "Whether he is a sinner or not, I don't know. One thing I do know. I was blind but now I see!"

26Then they asked him, "What did he do to you? How did he open your eyes?"

27He answered, "I have told you already and you did not listen. Why do you want to hear it again? Do you want to become his disciples, too?"

28Then they hurled insults at him and said, "You are this fellow's disciple! We are disciples of Moses! 29We know that God spoke to Moses, but as for this fellow, we don't even know where he comes from."

30The man answered, "Now that is remarkable! You don't know where he comes from, yet he opened my eyes. 31We know that God does not listen to sinners. He listens to the godly man who does his will. 32Nobody has ever heard of opening the eyes of a man born blind. 33If this man were not from God, he could do nothing."

34To this they replied, "You were steeped in sin at birth; how dare you lecture us!" And they threw him out.

Spiritual Blindness

35Jesus heard that they had thrown him out, and when he found him, he said, "Do you believe in the Son of Man?"

36"Who is he, sir?" the man asked. "Tell me so that I may believe in him."

37Jesus said, "You have now seen him; in fact, he is the one speaking with you."

38Then the man said, "Lord, I believe," and he worshiped him.

a22 Or *Messiah*   *b24* A solemn charge to tell the truth (see Joshua 7:19)

---

jealousy of Jesus' popularity and his influence on the people.

9:14–16 The Jewish Sabbath, Saturday, was the weekly holy day of rest. The Pharisees had made a long list of specific do's and don'ts regarding the Sabbath. Kneading the clay and healing the man were considered work and therefore were forbidden. Jesus may have made the clay in order to emphasize his teaching about the Sabbath—that it is right to care for others' needs even if it involves working on a day of rest.

●**9:25** By now the man who had been blind had heard the same questions over and over. He did not know how he was healed, but he knew that his life had been miraculously changed, and he was not afraid to tell the truth. You don't need to know all the answers in order to share Christ with others. It is important to tell them how he has changed your life. Then trust that God will use your words to help others believe in him too.

●**9:28, 34** The man's new faith was severely tested by some of the authorities. He was cursed and evicted from the temple. Persecution may come when you follow Jesus. You may lose friends; you may even lose your life. But no one can ever take away the eternal life Jesus gives you.

9:38 The longer this man experienced his new life through Christ, the more confident he became in the one who had healed him. He gained not only physical sight but also spiritual sight as he recognized Jesus first as a prophet (9:17), then as his Lord. When you turn to Christ, you begin to see him differently. The longer you walk with him, the better you understand who he is. Peter tells us to "grow in the grace and knowledge of our Lord and Savior Jesus Christ" (2 Peter 3:18). If you want to know more about Jesus, keep walking with him.

³⁹Jesus said, "For judgment I have come into this world, so that the blind will see and those who see will become blind."

9:39
Lk 4:18,19

⁴⁰Some Pharisees who were with him heard him say this and asked, "What? Are we blind too?"

9:40
Rom 2:19

⁴¹Jesus said, "If you were blind, you would not be guilty of sin; but now that you claim you can see, your guilt remains.

9:41
Prov 26:12
Jn 15:22

The Shepherd and His Flock

10 "I tell you the truth, the man who does not enter the sheep pen by the gate, but climbs in by some other way, is a thief and a robber. ²The man who enters by the gate is the shepherd of his sheep. ³The watchman opens the gate for him, and the sheep listen to his voice. He calls his own sheep by name and leads them out. ⁴When he has brought out all his own, he goes on ahead of them, and his sheep follow him because they know his voice. ⁵But they will never follow a stranger; in fact, they will run away from him because they do not recognize a stranger's voice." ⁶Jesus used this figure of speech, but they did not understand what he was telling them.

10:1
Isa 56:10
10:2
Acts 20:28

10:5
Prov 19:27
Gal 1:8
Eph 4:14
10:6
Jn 16:25
10:7
Jn 14:6

⁷Therefore Jesus said again, "I tell you the truth, I am the gate for the sheep. ⁸All who ever came before me were thieves and robbers, but the sheep did not listen to them. ⁹I am the gate; whoever enters through me will be saved.^a He will come in and go out, and find pasture. ¹⁰The thief comes only to steal and kill and destroy; I have come that they may have life, and have it to the full.

10:8
Jer 23:1; 50:6
Ezek 34:2
10:10
Jn 5:40
Acts 20:29
2 Pet 2:1

¹¹"I am the good shepherd. The good shepherd lays down his life for the sheep. ¹²The hired hand is not the shepherd who owns the sheep. So when he sees the wolf coming, he abandons the sheep and runs away. Then the wolf attacks the flock and scatters it. ¹³The man runs away because he is a hired hand and cares nothing for the sheep.

10:11
Isa 40:11
Ezek 34:11-16,
23; 37:24
Heb 13:20,21
1 Pet 2:25; 5:4
1 Jn 3:16
Rev 7:17

¹⁴"I am the good shepherd; I know my sheep and my sheep know me— ¹⁵just as the Father knows me and I know the Father—and I lay down my life for the sheep. ¹⁶I have other sheep that are not of this sheep pen. I must bring them also. They too will listen to my voice, and there shall be one flock and one shepherd. ¹⁷The reason my Father loves me is that I lay down my life—only to take it up again. ¹⁸No one takes it from me, but I lay it down of my own accord. I have authority to lay it down and authority to take it up again. This command I received from my Father."

10:14
Phil 3:10
2 Tim 2:19
10:16
Isa 56:6,7
Ezek 37:21,22
Jn 11:52
17:20-24
Eph 2:14; 3:6

10:17
Isa 53:6,7
2 Cor 5:15
Heb 2:9
1 Jn 3:16
10:18
Heb 5:8; 7:16

¹⁹At these words the Jews were again divided. ²⁰Many of them said, "He is demon-possessed and raving mad. Why listen to him?"

²¹But others said, "These are not the sayings of a man possessed by a demon. Can a demon open the eyes of the blind?"

^a9 Or kept safe

9:40, 41 The Pharisees were shocked that Jesus thought they were spiritually blind. Jesus countered that only blindness (stubbornness and stupidity) could excuse their behavior. To those who remained open (recognized how sin had truly blinded them from knowing the truth), he gave spiritual understanding and insight. But he rejected those who had become complacent, self-satisfied, and blind.

●**10:1** At night, sheep were often gathered into a sheep pen to protect them from thieves, weather, or wild animals. The sheep pens were caves, sheds, or open areas surrounded by walls made of stones or branches. The shepherd often slept in the pen to protect the sheep. Just as a shepherd cares for his sheep, Jesus, the good shepherd, cares for his flock (those who follow him). The prophet Ezekiel, in predicting the coming of the Messiah, called him a shepherd (Ezekiel 34:23).

10:10 In contrast to the thief who takes, Jesus gives. The life he gives now is abundantly richer and fuller. It is eternal, yet it begins immediately. Life in him is lived on a higher plain because of his overflowing forgiveness, love, and guidance.

●**10:11, 12** A hired hand tends the sheep for money, while the shepherd does it for love. The shepherd owns the sheep and is committed to them. Jesus is not merely doing a job; he is committed to love us and even lay down his life for us. False teachers and false prophets do not have this commitment.

●**10:16** The "other sheep" were non-Jews. Jesus came to save Gentiles as well as Jews. This is an insight into his worldwide mission—to die for the sins of the whole world. People tend to want to restrict God's blessings to their own group, but Jesus refuses to be limited by the fences we build.

10:17, 18 Jesus' death and resurrection, as part of God's plan for the salvation of the world, were under God's full control. No one could kill Jesus without his consent.

10:19, 20 If Jesus had been merely a man, his claims to be God would have proven him insane. But his miracles proved his words true—he really was God. The Jewish leaders could not see beyond their own prejudices, and they tried to put Jesus in a human box. But Jesus was not limited by their restricted vision.

The Unbelief of the Jews

10:23
Acts 3:11; 5:12
10:24
Lk 22:67

10:25
Jn 5:36
10:38; 14:10,11
10:26
Jn 8:47
1 Jn 4:6

22Then came the Feast of Dedication*a* at Jerusalem. It was winter, 23and Jesus was in the temple area walking in Solomon's Colonnade. 24The Jews gathered around him, saying, "How long will you keep us in suspense? If you are the Christ,*b* tell us plainly."

25Jesus answered, "I did tell you, but you do not believe. The miracles I do in my Father's name speak for me, 26but you do not believe because you are not my sheep. 27My sheep listen to my voice; I know them, and they follow me. 28I give them eternal life, and they shall never perish; no one can snatch them out of my

a22 That is, Hanukkah   b24 Or Messiah

THE NAMES OF JESUS
In different settings, Jesus gave himself names that pointed to special roles he was ready to fulfill for people. Some of these refer back to the Old Testament promises of the Messiah. Others were ways to help people understand him.

Reference	Name	Significance
6:27 (see textual note)	Son of Man	Jesus' favorite reference to himself. It emphasized his humanity—but the way he used it, it was a claim to divinity.
6:35	Bread of life	Refers to his life-giving role—that he is the only source of eternal life.
8:12	Light of the world	Light is a symbol of spiritual truth. Jesus is the universal answer for man's need of spiritual truth.
10:7	Gate for the sheep	Jesus is the only way into God's kingdom.
10:11	Good shepherd	Jesus appropriated the prophetic images of the Messiah pictured in the Old Testament. This is a claim to divinity, focusing on his love and guidance.
11:25	The one who raises the dead	Not only is Jesus the source of life, he is the power over death.
14:6	The way and the truth and the life	Jesus is the method, the message, and the meaning for all people. With this title he summarized his purpose in coming to earth.
15:5	The vine	This title has an important second part, "you are the branches." As in so many of his other names, Jesus reminds us that just as branches gain life from the vine and cannot live apart from it, so we are completely dependent on Christ for spiritual life.

10:22, 23 The Feast of Dedication commemorated the cleansing of the temple under Judas Maccabeus in 164 B.C., after Antiochus Epiphanes had defiled it by sacrificing a pig on the altar of burnt offering. It was celebrated toward the end of December. This is also the present-day Feast of Lights, Hanukkah.

10:23 Solomon's Colonnade was a roofed walkway supported by large stone columns, just inside the walls of the temple courtyard.

●**10:24** Many people asking for proof do so for the wrong reasons. Most of these questioners didn't want to follow Jesus in the way he wanted to lead them. They hoped he would declare himself Messiah for one of two other reasons. First, they, along with the disciples and everyone else in the Jewish nation, would have been delighted to have him drive out the Romans. Many of them didn't think he was going to do that, however. These doubters hoped he would identify himself so they could accuse him of telling lies (as the Pharisees did in 8:13).

10:28, 29 Just as a shepherd protects his sheep, Jesus protects his people from eternal harm. While believers can expect to suffer on earth, Satan cannot harm their souls or take away their eternal life with God. There are many reasons to be afraid here on earth, because this is Satan's domain. But if you choose to follow Jesus, he will give you everlasting safety.

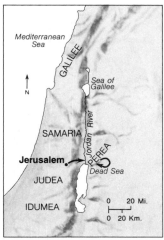

MINISTRY BEYOND THE JORDAN
Jesus had been in Jerusalem for the Feast of Tabernacles (7:2); then he preached in various towns, probably in Judea, before returning to Jerusalem for the Feast of Dedication. He again angered the religious leaders who tried to arrest him, but he left the city and went beyond the Jordan to preach.

hand. ²⁹My Father, who has given them to me, is greater than all*a*; no one can snatch them out of my Father's hand. ³⁰I and the Father are one."

³¹Again the Jews picked up stones to stone him, ³²but Jesus said to them, "I have shown you many great miracles from the Father. For which of these do you stone me?"

³³"We are not stoning you for any of these," replied the Jews, "but for blasphemy, because you, a mere man, claim to be God."

³⁴Jesus answered them, "Is it not written in your Law, 'I have said you are gods'*b*? ³⁵If he called them 'gods,' to whom the word of God came—and the Scripture cannot be broken— ³⁶what about the one whom the Father set apart as his very own and sent into the world? Why then do you accuse me of blasphemy because I said, 'I am God's Son'? ³⁷Do not believe me unless I do what my Father does. ³⁸But if I do it, even though you do not believe me, believe the miracles, that you may know and understand that the Father is in me, and I in the Father." ³⁹Again they tried to seize him, but he escaped their grasp.

⁴⁰Then Jesus went back across the Jordan to the place where John had been baptizing in the early days. Here he stayed ⁴¹and many people came to him. They said, "Though John never performed a miraculous sign, all that John said about this man was true." ⁴²And in that place many believed in Jesus.

10:28	Jn 6:37,39; 17:2,3; 1 Jn 5:11,12
10:29	Jn 14:28; 17:2,6
10:30	Jn 1:1; 10:38; 14:8-11; 17:21-24
10:33	Lev 24:15,16; Jn 1:1,18; 5:18; 20:28; Rom 9:5; Phil 2:6; Tit 2:13; 1 Jn 5:20
10:34	Ps 82:1,6
10:37	Jn 15:24
10:42	Jn 7:31; 8:30,31; 11:45

3. Jesus Encounters Crucial Events in Jerusalem

The Death of Lazarus

11 Now a man named Lazarus was sick. He was from Bethany, the village of Mary and her sister Martha. ²This Mary, whose brother Lazarus now lay sick, was the same one who poured perfume on the Lord and wiped his feet with her hair. ³So the sisters sent word to Jesus, "Lord, the one you love is sick."

⁴When he heard this, Jesus said, "This sickness will not end in death. No, it is for God's glory so that God's Son may be glorified through it." ⁵Jesus loved Martha

11:2 Mt 26:7; Mk 14:3; Lk 7:37,38; Jn 12:3

11:4 Jn 9:3

a29 Many early manuscripts What my Father has given me is greater than all b34 Psalm 82:6

10:30, 31 This is the clearest statement of Jesus' divinity he ever made. Jesus and his Father are not the same person, but they are one in essence and nature. Thus Jesus is not merely a good teacher—he is God. His claim to be God was unmistakable. The religious leaders wanted to kill him for it because their laws said that anyone claiming to be God should die. Nothing could persuade them that Jesus' claim was true.

10:31 The Jewish leaders attempted to carry out the direction found in Leviticus 24:16 regarding those who blaspheme (claim to be God). They intended to stone Jesus.

10:34-36 Jesus refers to Psalm 82:6 where the Israelite judges are called god (see also Exodus 4:16; 7:1). If God called the Israelite judges gods because they were the agents of God's revelation and will, how could it be blasphemy for Jesus to call himself the Son of God? Jesus was rebuking them because he is the Son of God in a unique, unparalleled relationship of oneness with the Father.

10:35 "The Scripture cannot be broken" is a clear statement of the truth of the Bible. If we accept Christ as Lord, we also accept his confirmation of the Bible as God's Word.

11:1 The village of Bethany was located about two miles east of Jerusalem on the road to Jericho. It was near enough to Jerusalem for them to be in danger, but far enough away so as not to attract attention prematurely.

11:3 As their brother grew very sick, Mary and Martha turned to Jesus for help. They believed in his ability to help because they had seen his miracles. We too know of his miracles, both from Scripture and through changed lives we have seen. When we need extraordinary help, Jesus offers extraordinary resources. We should not hesitate to ask him for help.

11:4 Any trial a believer faces can ultimately bring glory to God because God can bring good out of any bad situation. When trouble comes, do you grumble, complain, and blame God, or do you see your problems as opportunities to honor him?

JESUS RAISES LAZARUS
Jesus had been preaching in the villages beyond the Jordan, probably in Perea, when he received the news of Lazarus's sickness. Jesus did not leave immediately, but waited two days before returning to Judea. He knew Lazarus would be dead when he arrived in Bethany, but he was going to do a great miracle.

●11:5-7 Jesus loved this family and often stayed with them. He knew their pain but did not respond immediately. His delay had a specific purpose. God's timing, especially his delays, may make us think he is not answering or is not answering the way we want.

and her sister and Lazarus. 6Yet when he heard that Lazarus was sick, he stayed where he was two more days.

7Then he said to his disciples, "Let us go back to Judea."

8"But Rabbi," they said, "a short while ago the Jews tried to stone you, and yet you are going back there?"

9Jesus answered, "Are there not twelve hours of daylight? A man who walks by day will not stumble, for he sees by this world's light. 10It is when he walks by night that he stumbles, for he has no light."

11After he had said this, he went on to tell them, "Our friend Lazarus has fallen asleep; but I am going there to wake him up."

12His disciples replied, "Lord, if he sleeps, he will get better." 13Jesus had been speaking of his death, but his disciples thought he meant natural sleep.

14So then he told them plainly, "Lazarus is dead, 15and for your sake I am glad I was not there, so that you may believe. But let us go to him."

16Then Thomas (called Didymus) said to the rest of the disciples, "Let us also go, that we may die with him."

Jesus Comforts the Sisters

17On his arrival, Jesus found that Lazarus had already been in the tomb for four days. 18Bethany was less than two miles*a* from Jerusalem, 19and many Jews had come to Martha and Mary to comfort them in the loss of their brother. 20When Martha heard that Jesus was coming, she went out to meet him, but Mary stayed at home.

21"Lord," Martha said to Jesus, "if you had been here, my brother would not have died. 22But I know that even now God will give you whatever you ask."

23Jesus said to her, "Your brother will rise again."

24Martha answered, "I know he will rise again in the resurrection at the last day."

25Jesus said to her, "I am the resurrection and the life. He who believes in me will live, even though he dies; 26and whoever lives and believes in me will never die. Do you believe this?"

27"Yes, Lord," she told him, "I believe that you are the Christ,*b* the Son of God, who was to come into the world."

28And after she had said this, she went back and called her sister Mary aside. "The Teacher is here," she said, "and is asking for you." 29When Mary heard this, she got up quickly and went to him. 30Now Jesus had not yet entered the village, but was still at the place where Martha had met him. 31When the Jews who had been with Mary in the house, comforting her, noticed how quickly she got up and went out, they followed her, supposing she was going to the tomb to mourn there.

32When Mary reached the place where Jesus was and saw him, she fell at his feet and said, "Lord, if you had been here, my brother would not have died."

a18 Greek *fifteen stadia* (about 3 kilometers)   *b27* Or *Messiah*

Cross references (left margin):

11:8
Jn 8:59; 10:31

11:9
Ps 97:11
119:105,130
Prov 4:18; 13:9
Lk 13:33
Jn 9:4

11:10
Job 12:24,25
Jn 12:35
1 Jn 2:11

11:11
Dan 12:2
Acts 7:60
1 Cor 15:51

11:16
Mt 10:3
Jn 14:5
20:24-28; 21:2

11:17
Jn 11:39

11:20
Lk 10:38-42

11:22
Jn 9:31

11:23
Dan 12:2
Phil 3:21
1 Thess 4:14

11:24
Jn 5:28,29
Acts 24:15

11:25
Jn 1:4; 3:36
5:21; 6:39,40
14:6
Col 1:18; 3:4
1 Jn 1:1,2
5:10,11
Rev 1:17,18

11:26
Jn 6:47-51; 8:51

11:27
Mt 16:16
Jn 4:42
6:14,68,69

But he will meet all our needs according to his perfect schedule and purpose. Patiently await his timing.

11:9, 10 *Day* means the knowledge of God's will; *night* means absence of this knowledge. When we move ahead in darkness, we are likely to stumble.

11:14, 15 If Jesus had been with Lazarus during the final moments of his sickness, he might have healed him rather than let him die. But Lazarus died so that Jesus' power over death could be shown to his disciples and others. Jesus' delay was not for purposes of showmanship—to impress people. It was an essential display of his power and a major belief of Christian faith. He not only raised himself from the dead, but he has the power to raise others.

11:16 The disciples knew the dangers of going with Jesus to Jerusalem, and they tried to talk him out of it. Thomas merely expressed what all of them felt. When their objections failed, they were willing to go and even die with him. They may not have understood why Jesus would die, but they were loyal. There are unknown dangers in doing God's work. It is wise to consider the high cost of being Jesus' disciple.

11:25, 26 Jesus has power over life and death as well as power to forgive sins. This is because he is the Creator of life (see John 14:6). He who *is* life can surely restore life. Whoever believes in him has a spiritual life that death cannot touch or diminish in any way. When we realize his power and how wonderful his offer to us really is, how can we help but commit our lives to him! To those of us who believe, what wonderful assurance and certainty we have: "Because I live, you also will live" (14:19).

11:27 Martha is best known for being too busy to sit down and talk with Jesus (Luke 10:38–42). But here we see her as a woman of deep faith. Her statement of faith is exactly the response Jesus desires from us.

33When Jesus saw her weeping, and the Jews who had come along with her also weeping, he was deeply moved in spirit and troubled. 34"Where have you laid him?" he asked.

"Come and see, Lord," they replied.

35Jesus wept.

36Then the Jews said, "See how he loved him!"

37But some of them said, "Could not he who opened the eyes of the blind man have kept this man from dying?"

11:35
Isa 53:3
Lk 19:41
Rom 12:15
Heb 4:15
11:37
Jn 9:6,7

Jesus Raises Lazarus From the Dead

38Jesus, once more deeply moved, came to the tomb. It was a cave with a stone laid across the entrance. 39"Take away the stone," he said.

"But, Lord," said Martha, the sister of the dead man, "by this time there is a bad odor, for he has been there four days."

11:39
Jn 11:17

40Then Jesus said, "Did I not tell you that if you believed, you would see the glory of God?"

41So they took away the stone. Then Jesus looked up and said, "Father, I thank you that you have heard me. 42I knew that you always hear me, but I said this for the benefit of the people standing here, that they may believe that you sent me."

43When he had said this, Jesus called in a loud voice, "Lazarus, come out!" 44The dead man came out, his hands and feet wrapped with strips of linen, and a cloth around his face.

Jesus said to them, "Take off the grave clothes and let him go."

11:41
Mt 11:25; 27:60
Lk 24:2
11:42
Jn 12:30
11:43
Deut 32:39
1 Sam 2:6
Lk 7:14; 8:54
Acts 3:15; 9:40

The Plot to Kill Jesus

45Therefore many of the Jews who had come to visit Mary, and had seen what Jesus did, put their faith in him. 46But some of them went to the Pharisees and told them what Jesus had done. 47Then the chief priests and the Pharisees called a meeting of the Sanhedrin.

"What are we accomplishing?" they asked. "Here is this man performing many miraculous signs. 48If we let him go on like this, everyone will believe in him, and then the Romans will come and take away both our place*a* and our nation."

49Then one of them, named Caiaphas, who was high priest that year, spoke up, "You know nothing at all! 50You do not realize that it is better for you that one man die for the people than that the whole nation perish."

51He did not say this on his own, but as high priest that year he prophesied that Jesus would die for the Jewish nation, 52and not only for that nation but also for the scattered children of God, to bring them together and make them one. 53So from that day on they plotted to take his life.

54Therefore Jesus no longer moved about publicly among the Jews. Instead he

*a*48 Or temple

11:47
Ps 2:2
Jn 12:19
Acts 4:16
11:48
Dan 9:26,27
11:49
Mt 26:3
Lk 3:1,2
Acts 4:6
11:50
Jn 18:14
11:51
Ex 28:30
Num 27:21
Ezra 2:62,63
11:52
Jn 10:16
Eph 2:14-19; 3:6
1 Pet 5:9
11:53
Mt 26:3,4

11:33–38 John stresses that we have a God who cares. This contrasts with the Greek concept of God that was popular in his day—a God with no emotions and no messy involvement with humans. Here we see many of Jesus' emotions—compassion, indignation, sorrow, even frustration. He often expressed deep emotion, and we must never be afraid to reveal our true feelings to him. He understands them, for he experienced them. Be honest, and don't try to hide anything from your Savior. He cares.

•**11:35** When Jesus saw the weeping and wailing, he too wept openly. Perhaps he empathized with their grief, or perhaps he was troubled at their unbelief. In either case, Jesus showed that he cares enough for us to weep with us in sorrow.

11:38 Tombs at this time were usually caves carved in the limestone rock of a hillside. A tomb was often large enough for people to walk inside. Several bodies were usually placed in one tomb. After burial, a large stone was rolled across the entrance to the tomb.

11:44 Jesus raised others from the dead, including Jairus's daughter (Matthew 9:18–26; Mark 5:41, 42; Luke 8:40–56) and a widow's son (Luke 7:11–15).

11:45–53 Even when confronted point-blank with the power of Jesus' deity, some refused to believe. These eyewitnesses not only rejected him; they plotted his murder. They were so hardened that they preferred to reject God's Son rather than admit they were wrong. Beware of pride. If we allow it to grow, it can lead us into enormous sin.

11:48 The Jewish leaders knew if they didn't stop Jesus, the Romans would discipline them. Rome gave partial freedom to the Jews as long as they were quiet and obedient. Jesus' miracles often caused a disturbance. The leaders feared that Rome's displeasure would bring additional hardship to their nation.

11:51 John regarded Caiaphas's statement as a prophecy. As high priest, Caiaphas was used by God to explain Jesus' death even though Caiaphas didn't realize what he was doing.

withdrew to a region near the desert, to a village called Ephraim, where he stayed with his disciples.

11:55
Ex 19:10
2 Chron
30:17-19
Mt 26:1,2
Mk 14:1
Lk 22:1
Jn 18:28

55When it was almost time for the Jewish Passover, many went up from the country to Jerusalem for their ceremonial cleansing before the Passover. 56They kept looking for Jesus, and as they stood in the temple area they asked one another, "What do you think? Isn't he coming to the Feast at all?" 57But the chief priests and Pharisees had given orders that if anyone found out where Jesus was, he should report it so that they might arrest him.

Jesus Anointed at Bethany

12:1
Jn 11:43

12:3
Lk 10:38-41
Jn 11:1,2

12 Six days before the Passover, Jesus arrived at Bethany, where Lazarus lived, whom Jesus had raised from the dead. 2Here a dinner was given in Jesus' honor. Martha served, while Lazarus was among those reclining at the table with him. 3Then Mary took about a pint*a* of pure nard, an expensive perfume; she

a3 Greek a litra (probably about 0.5 liter)

Caiaphas was the leader of the religious group called the Sadducees. Educated and wealthy, they were the political rulers of the nation. As the elite group, they were on fairly good terms with Rome. They hated Jesus because he endangered their secure lifestyles and taught a message they could not accept. A kingdom in which leaders *served* had no appeal to them.

Caiaphas's usual policy was to remove any threats to his power by whatever means necessary. For Caiaphas, whether Jesus should die was not in question; the only point to be settled was *when* his death should take place. Not only did Jesus have to be captured and tried; the Jewish council also needed Roman approval before they could carry out the death sentence. Caiaphas's plans were unexpectedly helped by Judas's offer to betray Christ.

Caiaphas did not realize that his schemes were actually part of a wonderful plan God was carrying out. Caiaphas's willingness to sacrifice another man to preserve his own security was clearly selfish. By contrast, Jesus' willingness to die for us was a clear example of loving self-sacrifice. Caiaphas thought he had won the battle as Jesus hung on the cross, but he did not count on the resurrection!

Caiaphas's mind was closed. He couldn't accept the resurrection even when the evidence was overwhelming, and he attempted to silence those whose lives had been forever changed by the risen Christ (Matthew 28:12, 13). Caiaphas represents those people who will not believe because they think it will cost them too much to accept Jesus as Lord. They choose the fleeting power, prestige, and pleasures of this life instead of the eternal life God offers those who receive his Son. What is your choice?

Strength and accomplishment:
* High priest for 18 years

Weaknesses and mistakes:
* One of those most directly responsible for Jesus' death
* Used his office as a means to power and personal security
* Planned Jesus' capture, carried out his illegal trial, pressured Pilate to approve the crucifixion, attempted to prevent the resurrection, and later tried to cover up the fact of the resurrection
* Kept up religious appearances while compromising with Rome
* Involved in the later persecution of Christians

Lessons from his life:
* God uses even the perverse intentions of his enemies to bring about his will
* When we cover selfish motives with spiritual objectives and words, God still sees our intentions

Vital statistics:
* Where: Jerusalem
* Occupation: High priest
* Relatives: Father-in-law: Annas
* Contemporaries: Jesus, Pilate, Herod Antipas

Key verses:
"Then one of them, named Caiaphas, who was high priest that year, spoke up, 'You know nothing at all! You do not realize that it is better for you that one man die for the people than that the whole nation perish'" (John 11:49, 50).

12:3 Pure nard was a fragrant ointment imported from the mountains of India. Thus it was very expensive. The amount Mary used was worth a year's wages. Nard was used to anoint kings; Mary may have been anointing Jesus as her kingly Messiah.

poured it on Jesus' feet and wiped his feet with her hair. And the house was filled with the fragrance of the perfume.

4But one of his disciples, Judas Iscariot, who was later to betray him, objected, 5"Why wasn't this perfume sold and the money given to the poor? It was worth a year's wages. *a* " 6He did not say this because he cared about the poor but because he was a thief; as keeper of the money bag, he used to help himself to what was put into it.

7"Leave her alone," Jesus replied. "It was intended, that she should save this perfume for the day of my burial. 8You will always have the poor among you, but you will not always have me."

9Meanwhile a large crowd of Jews found out that Jesus was there and came, not only because of him but also to see Lazarus, whom he had raised from the dead. 10So the chief priests made plans to kill Lazarus as well, 11for on account of him many of the Jews were going over to Jesus and putting their faith in him.

The Triumphal Entry

12The next day the great crowd that had come for the Feast heard that Jesus was on his way to Jerusalem. 13They took palm branches and went out to meet him, shouting,

"Hosanna! *b* "

"Blessed is he who comes in the name of the Lord!" *c*

"Blessed is the King of Israel!"

14Jesus found a young donkey and sat upon it, as it is written,

a5 Greek three hundred denarii   *b13 A Hebrew expression meaning "Save!" which became an exclamation of praise   *c13 Psalm 118:25, 26*

12:4
Jn 6:70,71

12:6
Prov 28:20,22
Jn 13:29
1 Cor 5:10,11
6:10
Eph 5:5
1 Tim 6:9,10

12:7
Mt 26:10-13
Mk 14:8,9
Jn 19:40

12:8
Deut 15:11
Mk 14:7

12:10
Lk 16:31

12:12
Mt 21:4-9
Mk 11:7-10
Lk 19:35-38

12:13
Ps 118:26
1 Tim 1:17

TIME WITH THE DISCIPLES

Lazarus's return to life became the last straw for the religious leaders who were bent on killing Jesus. So Jesus stopped his public ministry and took his disciples away from Jerusalem to Ephraim. From there they returned to Galilee for a while (see the map in Luke 17:11).

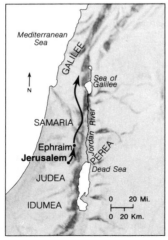

Mediterranean Sea

GALILEE

N

Sea of Galilee

SAMARIA

Jordan River

Ephraim
Jerusalem

PEREA

Dead Sea

JUDEA

IDUMEA

0   20 Mi.

0   20 Km.

12:4–6 Judas often dipped into the disciples' funds for his own use. Jesus, of course, knew this, but apparently never did or said anything about it. Similarly, when we choose the way of sin, God may not immediately do anything to stop us, but this does not mean he approves our actions. What we deserve will come.

12:5, 6 Judas used a pious phrase to hide his true motives. But Jesus knew what was in his heart. His life had become a lie and Satan was entering his heart (13:27). Satan is the father of lies and a lying character opens the door to his influence. Jesus' knowledge of us should make us want to keep our actions consistent with our words. Since we have nothing to fear with him, we should have nothing to hide.

12:7, 8 This act and Jesus' response to it do not teach us to ignore the poor so we can spend money extravagantly for Christ. This was a unique act for a specific occasion—an anointing for Jesus' burial and a public declaration of faith in him as Messiah. Jesus' words should have taught Judas a valuable lesson about the worth of money. Unfortunately, Judas did not take heed; soon he would sell his Master's life for 30 pieces of silver.

12:10, 11 The chief priests' blindness and hardness of heart caused them to sink ever deeper into sin. They rejected the Messiah, planned to kill him, and now plotted to murder Lazarus also. One sin leads to another. From the Jewish leaders' point of view, they could accuse Jesus of blasphemy because he claimed equality with God. But Lazarus had done nothing of the kind. They wanted him dead simply because he was a living witness to Jesus' power. This is a warning to us to avoid sin. Sin leads to more sin, a downward spiral that can be stopped only by repentance and the power of the Holy Spirit to change our behavior.

●**12:13** Jesus began his last week on earth by riding into Jerusalem on a donkey under a canopy of palm branches, with crowds hailing him as their king. To announce that he was indeed the Messiah, Jesus chose a *time* when all Israel would be gathered at Jerusalem, a *place* where huge crowds could see him, and a *way* of proclaiming his mission that was unmistakable. On Palm Sunday we celebrate Jesus' triumphal entry into Jerusalem.

12:13 The people who were praising God for giving them a king had the wrong idea about Jesus. They were sure he would be a national leader who would restore their nation to its former glory, and thus they were deaf to the words of their prophets and blind to Jesus' real mission. When it became apparent that Jesus was not going to fulfill their hopes, many people turned against him.

●**12:16** After Jesus' resurrection, the disciples understood for the first time many of the prophecies that they had missed along the way. Jesus' words and actions took on new meaning and made more sense. In retrospect, they saw how Jesus had led them into a deeper and better understanding of his truth. Stop now and think

12:15
Zech 9:9

> 15"Do not be afraid, O Daughter of Zion;
>> see, your king is coming,
>> seated on a donkey's colt."*a*

16At first his disciples did not understand all this. Only after Jesus was glorified did they realize that these things had been written about him and that they had done these things to him.

12:17
Jn 11:42
12:18
Jn 12:11

17Now the crowd that was with him when he called Lazarus from the tomb and raised him from the dead continued to spread the word. 18Many people, because they had heard that he had given this miraculous sign, went out to meet him. 19So the Pharisees said to one another, "See, this is getting us nowhere. Look how the whole world has gone after him!"

Jesus Predicts His Death

12:21
Jn 1:43,44
12:23,24
Jn 13:32; 17:1
Rom 6:4,5
1 Cor 15:36-45
12:25
Lk 9:24; 17:33

20Now there were some Greeks among those who went up to worship at the Feast. 21They came to Philip, who was from Bethsaida in Galilee, with a request. "Sir," they said, "we would like to see Jesus." 22Philip went to tell Andrew; Andrew and Philip in turn told Jesus.

23Jesus replied, "The hour has come for the Son of Man to be glorified. 24I tell you the truth, unless a kernel of wheat falls to the ground and dies, it remains only a single seed. But if it dies, it produces many seeds. 25The man who loves his life

a15 Zech. 9:9

GREAT EXPECTATIONS Wherever he went, Jesus exceeded people's expectations.	What was expected	What Jesus did	Reference
	A man looked for healing	Jesus also forgave his sins	Mark 2:1−12
	The disciples were expecting an ordinary day of fishing	They found the Savior	Luke 5:1−11
	A widow was resigned to bury her dead son	Jesus restored her son to life	Luke 7:11−17
	The religious leaders wanted a miracle	Jesus offered them the Creator of miracles	Matthew 12:38−45
	A woman who wanted to be healed touched Jesus	Jesus helped her see it was her faith that had healed her	Mark 5:25−34
	The disciples thought the crowd should be sent home because there was no food	Jesus used a small meal to feed thousands, and there were leftovers!	John 6:1−15
	The crowds looked for a political leader to set up a new kingdom to overthrow Rome's control	Jesus offered them an eternal, spiritual kingdom to overthrow sin's control	A theme throughout the Gospels
	The disciples wanted to eat the Passover meal with Jesus, their Lord	Jesus washed their feet, showing he was also their servant	John 13:1−20
	The religious leaders wanted Jesus killed and got their wish	But Jesus rose from the dead!	John 11:53; 19:30; 20:1−29

about the events in your life leading up to where you are now. How has God led you to this point? As you grow older, you will look back and see God's involvement more clearly than you do now.

12:18 The people flocked to Jesus because they had heard of his great miracle in raising Lazarus from the dead. Their adoration was short-lived and their commitment shallow, for in a few days they would do nothing to stop his crucifixion. Devotion based only on curiosity or popularity fades quickly.

12:20, 21 These Greeks were converts to the Jewish faith. They probably went to Philip because, though he was a Jew, he had a Greek name.

12:23−25 This is a beautiful picture of the necessary sacrifice of Jesus. Unless a kernel of wheat is buried, it will not become a

blade of wheat producing many more seeds. Jesus had to die to pay the penalty for our sin, and also to show his power over death. His resurrection proves he has eternal life. Because he is God, he can give this same eternal life to all who believe in him.

12:25 We must be so committed to living for Christ that we "hate" our lives by comparison. This does not mean that we long to die or are careless or destructive with the life God has given, but that we are willing to die if doing so will glorify Christ. We must disown the tyrannical rule of our own self-centeredness. By laying aside our striving for advantage, security, and pleasure, we can serve God lovingly and freely. Releasing control of our life and transferring control to Jesus brings eternal life and genuine joy in the present.

will lose it, while the man who hates his life in this world will keep it for eternal life. 26Whoever serves me must follow me; and where I am, my servant also will be. My Father will honor the one who serves me.

27"Now my heart is troubled, and what shall I say? 'Father, save me from this hour'? No, it was for this very reason I came to this hour. 28Father, glorify your name!"

Then a voice came from heaven, "I have glorified it, and will glorify it again." 29The crowd that was there and heard it said it had thundered; others said an angel had spoken to him.

30Jesus said, "This voice was for your benefit, not mine. 31Now is the time for judgment on this world; now the prince of this world will be driven out. 32But I, when I am lifted up from the earth, will draw all men to myself." 33He said this to show the kind of death he was going to die.

34The crowd spoke up, "We have heard from the Law that the Christ*a* will remain forever, so how can you say, 'The Son of Man must be lifted up'? Who is this 'Son of Man'?"

35Then Jesus told them, "You are going to have the light just a little while longer. Walk while you have the light, before darkness overtakes you. The man who walks in the dark does not know where he is going. 36Put your trust in the light while you have it, so that you may become sons of light." When he had finished speaking, Jesus left and hid himself from them.

The Jews Continue in Their Unbelief

37Even after Jesus had done all these miraculous signs in their presence, they still would not believe in him. 38This was to fulfill the word of Isaiah the prophet:

> "Lord, who has believed our message
> and to whom has the arm of the Lord been revealed?"*b*

39For this reason they could not believe, because, as Isaiah says elsewhere:

a34 Or *Messiah*   *b38* Isaiah 53:1

12:27
Lk 12:50; 22:53

12:28
Mt 3:17; 17:5
Mk 1:11; 9:7
Lk 3:22; 9:35
2 Pet 1:17,18

12:31
Jn 14:30; 16:11
Eph 6:12
Heb 2:14

12:32
Jn 3:14; 6:44

12:34
2 Sam 7:13
Ps 89:35,36
110:4
Isa 9:7
Dan 7:14

12:35
Jer 13:16
Jn 8:12; 9:5
12:46

12:36
Lk 16:8
Jn 8:12; 12:46
Eph 5:8
1 Thess 5:5
1 Jn 2:9,10

12:38
Isa 53:1
Rom 10:16

12:26 Many believed that Jesus came for the Jews only. But when Jesus said, "whoever serves me must follow me," he was talking to these Greeks. No matter who the sincere seekers are, Jesus welcomes them. His message is for everyone. Don't allow social or racial differences to become barriers to the gospel. Take the Word to all people.

●**12:27** Jesus knew his crucifixion lay ahead, and because he was human he dreaded it. He knew he would have to take the sins of the world on himself, and he knew this would separate him from his Father. He wanted to be delivered from this horrible death, but he knew that God sent him into the world to die for our sins, in our place. Jesus said no to his human desires in order to obey his Father and bring glory to him. Although we will never have to face such a difficult task, we are still called to obedience. Whatever the Father asks, we should do his will and bring glory to his name.

●**12:31** The prince of this world was Satan, an angel who rebelled against God. He is real, not symbolic, and is constantly working against God and those who obey him. He tempted Eve in the garden and persuaded her to sin; he tempted Jesus in the desert and did not persuade him to fall (Matthew 4:1–11). Satan has great power, but people can be delivered from his reign of spiritual darkness because of Christ's victory on the cross. Satan is powerful, but Jesus is much more powerful. Jesus' resurrection shattered Satan's deathly power (Colossians 1:13, 14). To overcome Satan we need faithful allegiance to God's Word, determination to stay away from sin, and the support of other believers.

12:32–34 The crowd could not believe the Messiah would die. They were waving palm branches for a victorious Messiah who they thought would set up a political, earthly kingdom that would never end. From their reading of certain Scriptural passages, they

thought the Messiah would never die (Psalms 89:35, 36; 110:4; Isaiah 9:7). Other passages, however, showed that he would (Isaiah 53:5–9). Jesus' words did not fit their concept of the Messiah. First he had to suffer and die—then he would one day set up his eternal kingdom. For what kind of Messiah, or Savior, are you looking? Beware of trying to force Jesus into your own mold—he won't fit.

12:35, 36 Jesus said he would be with them in person for only a short time, and they should take advantage of his presence while they had it. Like a light in a dark place, he would show them where to go. If they walked in his light, they would become "sons of light," revealing the truth and pointing people to God. As Christians, we are to be Christ's light bearers, letting his light shine through us. How brightly is your light shining? Can others see Christ in your actions?

12:37, 38 Jesus had performed many miracles, but most people still didn't believe in him. Likewise, many today won't believe despite all God does. Don't be discouraged if your witness for Christ doesn't turn as many to him as you'd like. Your job is to continue as a faithful witness. You are responsible to reach out to others, but they are responsible for their own decisions.

12:39–41 People in Jesus' time, like those in the time of Isaiah, would not believe despite the evidence (12:37). As a result, God "deadened" or hardened their hearts. Does that mean God intentionally prevented these people from believing in him? No, he simply confirmed their own choices. After a lifetime of resisting God, they had become so set in their ways that they wouldn't even try to understand Jesus' message. For such people, it is virtually impossible to come to God—their hearts have been permanently hardened. Other instances of hardened hearts because of constant stubbornness are recorded in Exodus 9:12, Romans 1:24–28, and 2 Thessalonians 2:8–12.

12:40
Isa 6:9,10
Mt 13:14

40"He has blinded their eyes
    and deadened their hearts,
so they can neither see with their eyes,
    nor understand with their hearts,
    nor turn—and I would heal them."*a*

12:41
Isa 6:1

41Isaiah said this because he saw Jesus' glory and spoke about him.

12:42
Jn 7:13,48
9:22,23; 12:11

42Yet at the same time many even among the leaders believed in him. But because of the Pharisees they would not confess their faith for fear they would be put out of the synagogue; 43for they loved praise from men more than praise from God.

12:43
Jn 5:44

44Then Jesus cried out, "When a man believes in me, he does not believe in me only, but in the one who sent me. 45When he looks at me, he sees the one who sent me. 46I have come into the world as a light, so that no one who believes in me should stay in darkness.

12:45
Jn 14:9

12:46
Jn 1:4,5,9
3:19; 8:12
9:5,39

47"As for the person who hears my words but does not keep them, I do not judge him. For I did not come to judge the world, but to save it. 48There is a judge for the one who rejects me and does not accept my words; that very word which I spoke will condemn him at the last day. 49For I did not speak of my own accord, but the Father who sent me commanded me what to say and how to say it. 50I know that his command leads to eternal life. So whatever I say is just what the Father has told me to say."

12:47
Jn 3:17; 5:45
8:15,16

12:48
Deut 18:18,19

C. DEATH AND RESURRECTION OF JESUS, THE SON OF GOD (13:1—21:25)

John begins his Gospel with eternity and ends with Jesus coming to earth again. He features Jesus teaching his disciples privately just before his arrest and death. We see, clearly, the deep love Jesus has for the believer, and the peace that comes from faith. Knowing the love Jesus has for believers, we too should believe and allow Jesus to forgive our sins. Only then will we experience peace in a world filled with turmoil.

1. Jesus Teaches His Disciples

Jesus Washes His Disciples' Feet

13:1
Jn 3:35; 16:28
17:2
1 Cor 15:27

13 It was just before the Passover Feast. Jesus knew that the time had come for him to leave this world and go to the Father. Having loved his own who were in the world, he now showed them the full extent of his love. *b*

2The evening meal was being served, and the devil had already prompted Judas

a40 Isaiah 6:10   *b1* Or *he loved them to the last*

12:42, 43 Along with those who refused to believe, many believed but refused to admit it. This is just as bad, and Jesus had strong words for such people (see Matthew 10:32, 33). People who do this are afraid of rejection or ridicule. Many Jewish leaders wouldn't admit to faith in Jesus because they feared excommunication from the synagogue (which was their livelihood) and loss of their prestigious place in the community. But the praise of others is fickle and short-lived. We should be concerned much more about God's eternal acceptance than the temporary approval of other people.

12:45 We often wonder what God is like. How can we know the Creator when he doesn't make himself visible? Jesus said plainly that those who see him see God, because he *is* God. If you want to know what God is like, study the person and words of Jesus Christ.

12:48 The purpose of Jesus' first mission on earth was not to judge people, but to show them the way to find salvation and eternal life. When he comes again, one of his main purposes will be to judge people for how they lived on earth. On the day of judgment, those who accepted Jesus and lived his way will be raised to eternal life (1 Corinthians 15:51–57; 1 Thessalonians 4:15–18; Revelation 21:1–8), and those who rejected Jesus and lived any way they pleased will face eternal punishment (Revelation 20:11–15). Decide now which side you'll be on, for the consequences of your decision last forever.

●13:1ff Chapters 13—17 tell us what Jesus said to his disciples the night before his death. These words were all spoken in one evening when, with only the disciples as his audience, he gave final instructions to prepare them for his death and resurrection, events that would change their lives forever.

13:1 Jesus knew he would be betrayed by one of his disciples, denied by another, and deserted by all of them for a time. Still "he now showed them the full extent of his love." God knows us completely, as Jesus knew his disciples. He knows the sins we have committed and the ones we will yet commit. Still, he loves us. How do you respond to that kind of love?

13:1–3 For more information on Judas Iscariot, see his Profile in Mark 14.

●13:1–17 Jesus was the model servant, and he showed this attitude to his disciples. Washing guests' feet was a job for a household servant when guests arrived. But Jesus wrapped a towel around him, as the lowliest slave would do, and washed his disciples' feet. If even he, God in the flesh, is willing to serve, we his followers must also be servants, willing to serve in any way that glorifies God. Are you willing to follow Christ's example of serving? Whom can you serve today? There is a special blessing for those who not only agree that humble service is Christ's way, but also follow through and do it (13:17).

Iscariot, son of Simon, to betray Jesus. 3Jesus knew that the Father had put all things under his power, and that he had come from God and was returning to God; 4so he got up from the meal, took off his outer clothing, and wrapped a towel around his waist. 5After that, he poured water into a basin and began to wash his disciples' feet, drying them with the towel that was wrapped around him.

6He came to Simon Peter, who said to him, "Lord, are you going to wash my feet?"

7Jesus replied, "You do not realize now what I am doing, but later you will understand."

8"No," said Peter, "you shall never wash my feet."

Jesus answered, "Unless I wash you, you have no part with me."

9"Then, Lord," Simon Peter replied, "not just my feet but my hands and my head as well!"

10Jesus answered, "A person who has had a bath needs only to wash his feet; his whole body is clean. And you are clean, though not every one of you." 11For he knew who was going to betray him, and that was why he said not every one was clean.

12When he had finished washing their feet, he put on his clothes and returned to his place. "Do you understand what I have done for you?" he asked them. 13"You call me 'Teacher' and 'Lord,' and rightly so, for that is what I am. 14Now that I, your Lord and Teacher, have washed your feet, you also should wash one another's feet. 15I have set you an example that you should do as I have done for you. 16I tell you the truth, no servant is greater than his master, nor is a messenger greater than the one who sent him. 17Now that you know these things, you will be blessed if you do them.

Jesus Predicts His Betrayal

18"I am not referring to all of you; I know those I have chosen. But this is to fulfill the scripture: 'He who shares my bread has lifted up his heel against me.' *a*

19"I am telling you now before it happens, so that when it does happen you will believe that I am He. 20I tell you the truth, whoever accepts anyone I send accepts me; and whoever accepts me accepts the one who sent me."

21After he had said this, Jesus was troubled in spirit and testified, "I tell you the truth, one of you is going to betray me."

22His disciples stared at one another, at a loss to know which of them he meant. 23One of them, the disciple whom Jesus loved, was reclining next to him. 24Simon Peter motioned to this disciple and said, "Ask him which one he means."

25Leaning back against Jesus, he asked him, "Lord, who is it?"

26Jesus answered, "It is the one to whom I will give this piece of bread when I have dipped it in the dish." Then, dipping the piece of bread, he gave it to Judas Iscariot, son of Simon. 27As soon as Judas took the bread, Satan entered into him.

a18 Psalm 41:9

13:2
Lk 22:3
Jn 6:70,71
13:4
Lk 12:37; 22:27
13:5
Lk 7:44
13:8
Ps 51:2,7
Isa 52:14,15
Ezek 36:25
Jn 3:5
Acts 2:38
1 Cor 6:11
Eph 5:26
Tit 3:5
Heb 9:13,14
10:22
13:10
Ex 29:4
30:18-21; 40:12
Jn 15:3
13:11
Jn 6:64; 13:2
13:13
1 Cor 8:6; 12:3
13:14
Lk 22:27
Rom 12:10
1 Pet 5:5
13:15
Phil 2:5-7
1 Pet 5:3-5
1 Jn 2:6
13:17
Jas 1:25
13:18
Ps 41:9
2 Tim 2:19
13:20
Mt 10:40
Lk 10:16
13:21
Mt 26:20-25
Mk 14:18-21
Lk 22:21-23
13:23
Jn 19:26
13:25
Jn 21:20
13:26
Jn 6:71
13:27
Lk 22:3

●**13:6, 7** Imagine being Peter and watching Jesus wash the others' feet, moving closer to you. Seeing his Master behave like a slave must have confused him. He still did not understand Jesus' teaching that to be a leader, one must be a servant. This is not a comfortable passage for leaders who find it hard to serve those under them. How do you treat those who work under you (whether children, employees, or volunteers)?

●**13:12ff** Jesus did not wash his disciples' feet just to get them to be nice to each other. His far greater goal was to extend his mission on earth after he was gone. They were to move into the world serving God, serving each other, and serving all people to whom they took the message of salvation.

13:26 The honored guest at a meal was singled out in this way.

13:27 Satan's part in the betrayal of Jesus does not remove any of the responsibility from Judas. Disillusioned because Jesus was talking about dying rather than setting up his kingdom, Judas may have been trying to force his hand and make him use his power to prove he was the Messiah. Or perhaps Judas, not understanding Jesus' mission, no longer believed he was God's chosen one. Whatever Judas thought, Satan assumed that Jesus' death would end his mission and thwart God's plan. Like Judas, he did not know Jesus' death was the most important part of God's plan all along.

13:27-38 John describes these few moments in clear detail. We can see that Jesus knew exactly what was going to happen. He knew about Judas and about Peter, but he did not change the situation, nor did he stop loving them. In the same way, Jesus knows exactly what you will do to hurt him. Yet he still loves you unconditionally and will forgive you whenever you ask for it. Judas couldn't understand this, and his life ended tragically. Peter understood, and despite his shortcomings, his life ended triumphantly because he never let go of his faith.

"What you are about to do, do quickly," Jesus told him, 28but no one at the meal understood why Jesus said this to him. 29Since Judas had charge of the money, some thought Jesus was telling him to buy what was needed for the Feast, or to give something to the poor. 30As soon as Judas had taken the bread, he went out. And it was night.

13:29
Jn 12:6

13:30
Lk 22:53

Jesus Predicts Peter's Denial

13:31,32
Lk 24:26
Jn 12:23; 17:1,5
1 Cor 15:42
Heb 5:5

13:33
Jn 7:33,34

31When he was gone, Jesus said, "Now is the Son of Man glorified and God is glorified in him. 32If God is glorified in him, *a* God will glorify the Son in himself, and will glorify him at once.

33"My children, I will be with you only a little longer. You will look for me, and just as I told the Jews, so I tell you now: Where I am going, you cannot come.

a32 Many early manuscripts do not have If God is glorified in him.

Being loved is the most powerful motivation in the world! Our ability to love is often shaped by our experience of love. We usually love others as we have been loved.

Some of the greatest statements about God's loving nature were written by a man who experienced God's love in a unique way. John, Jesus' disciple, expressed his relationship to the Son of God by calling himself "the disciple whom Jesus loved" (John 21:20). Although Jesus' love is clearly communicated in all the Gospels, in John's Gospel it is a central theme. Because his own experience of Jesus' love was so strong and personal, John was sensitive to those words and actions of Jesus that illustrated how the one who *is* love loved others.

Jesus knew John fully and loved him fully. He gave John and his brother James the nickname "Sons of Thunder," perhaps from an occasion when the brothers asked Jesus for permission to "call fire down from heaven" (Luke 9:54) on a village that had refused to welcome Jesus and the disciples. In John's Gospel and letters, we see the great God of love, while the thunder of God's justice bursts from the pages of Revelation.

Jesus confronts each of us as he confronted John. We cannot know the depth of his love unless we are willing to face the fact that he knows us completely. Otherwise we are fooled into believing he must love the people we pretend to be, not the sinners we actually are. John and all the disciples convince us that God is able and willing to accept us as we are. Being aware of God's love is a great motivator for change. His love is not given in exchange for our efforts; his love frees us to really live. Have you accepted that love?

Strengths and accomplishments:
● Before following Jesus, one of John the Baptist's disciples
● One of the 12 disciples and, with Peter and James, one of the inner three, closest to Jesus
● Wrote five New Testament books: the Gospel of John; 1, 2, and 3 John; and Revelation

Weaknesses and mistakes:
● Along with James, shared a tendency to outbursts of selfishness and anger
● Asked for a special position in Jesus' kingdom

Lessons from his life:
● Those who realize how much they are loved are able to love much
● When God changes a life, he does not take away personality characteristics, but puts them to effective use in his service

Vital statistics:
● Occupation: Fisherman, disciple
● Relatives: Father: Zebedee. Mother: Salome. Brother: James
● Contemporaries: Jesus, Pilate, Herod

Key verses:
"Dear friends, I am not writing you a new command but an old one, which you have had since the beginning. This old command is the message you have heard. Yet I am writing you a new command; its truth is seen in him and you, because the darkness is passing and the true light is already shining" (1 John 2:7, 8).

John's story is told throughout the Gospels, Acts, and Revelation.

34"A new command I give you: Love one another. As I have loved you, so you must love one another. 35By this all men will know that you are my disciples, if you love one another."

13:34
Lev 19:18
Eph 5:2
1 Thess 4:9
Heb 13:1
Jas 2:8
1 Pet 1:22
1 Jn 2:8; 3:11
4:20,21

36Simon Peter asked him, "Lord, where are you going?"

Jesus replied, "Where I am going, you cannot follow now, but you will follow later."

37Peter asked, "Lord, why can't I follow you now? I will lay down my life for you."

13:35
Acts 2:44-46

38Then Jesus answered, "Will you really lay down your life for me? I tell you the truth, before the rooster crows, you will disown me three times!

13:36
Jn 14:2; 21:18
2 Pet 1:13,14

Jesus Comforts His Disciples

14 "Do not let your hearts be troubled. Trust in God*a*; trust also in me. 2In my Father's house are many rooms; if it were not so, I would have told you. I am going there to prepare a place for you. 3And if I go and prepare a place for you, I will come back and take you to be with me that you also may be where I am. 4You know the way to the place where I am going."

14:2
Ps 90:1
Jn 2:16,19-21

14:3
Jn 10:38
16:16,19-22
17:21-24

Jesus the Way to the Father

5Thomas said to him, "Lord, we don't know where you are going, so how can we know the way?"

6Jesus answered, "I am the way and the truth and the life. No one comes to the Father except through me. 7If you really knew me, you would know*b* my Father as well. From now on, you do know him and have seen him."

14:6
Jn 1:4,14,16·
8:32; 10:9,10
11:25

14:7
Jn 6:46; 8:19
1 Jn 2:13

8Philip said, "Lord, show us the Father and that will be enough for us."

9Jesus answered: "Don't you know me, Philip, even after I have been among you such a long time? Anyone who has seen me has seen the Father. How can you say, 'Show us the Father'? 10Don't you believe that I am in the Father, and that the Father is in me? The words I say to you are not just my own. Rather, it is the Father, living in me, who is doing his work. 11Believe me when I say that I am in the Father

14:9
Jn 1:14,18
2 Cor 4:4
Col 1:15

14:10
Jn 5:19; 10:38
17:11,21-24

a1 Or You trust in God   b7 Some early manuscripts If you really have known me, you will know

---

13:34 To love others was not a new commandment (see Leviticus 19:18), but to love others as much as Christ loved others was revolutionary. Now we are to love others based on Jesus' sacrificial love for us. Such love will not only bring unbelievers to Christ; it will also keep believers strong and united in a world hostile to God. Jesus was a living example of God's love, as we are to be living examples of Jesus' love.

13:34, 35 Jesus says that our Christlike love will show we are his disciples. Do people see petty bickering, jealousy, and division in your church? Or do they know you are Jesus' followers by your love for one another?

13:35 Love is not simply warm feelings; it is instead an attitude that reveals itself in action. How can we love others as Jesus loves us? By helping when it's not convenient, by giving when it hurts, by devoting energy to others' welfare rather than our own, by absorbing hurts from others without complaining or fighting back. This kind of loving is hard to do. That is why people notice when you do it and know you are empowered by a supernatural source. The Bible has another beautiful description of love in 1 Corinthians 13.

13:37, 38 Peter proudly told Jesus that he was ready to die for him. But Jesus corrected him. He knew Peter would deny him that very night to protect himself (18:25–27). In our enthusiasm, it is easy to make promises, but God knows the extent of our commitment. Paul tells us that it's better to value ourselves more highly than we ought (Romans 12:3). Instead of bragging, show your commitment step by step as you grow in your knowledge of God's Word and in your faith.

14:1–3 Jesus' words show that the way to eternal life, though un-

seen, is certain—as assured as your trust in Jesus. He has already prepared the way to eternal life. The only issue that may still be unsettled is your willingness to believe.

14:2, 3 There are few verses in Scripture that describe eternal life, but they are rich with promises. Here Jesus says, "I am going there to prepare a place for you," and "I will come back." We can look forward to eternal life because Jesus has promised it to all who believe in him. Although the details of eternity are unknown, we need not fear, because Jesus is preparing for us and will spend eternity with us.

14:5, 6 This is one of the most basic and important passages in Scripture. How can we know the way to God? Only through Jesus. Jesus is the way because he is both God and man. By uniting our lives with his, we are united with God. Trust Jesus to take you to the Father, and all the benefits of being God's child will be yours.

14:6 Jesus says he is the *only* way to God the Father. Some people may argue that this is too narrow. In reality, it is wide enough for the whole world, if the world chooses to accept it. Instead of worrying about how limited it sounds to have only one way, we should be saying, "Thank you, God, for providing a sure way to get to you!"

14:6 As the *way,* Jesus is our path to the Father. As the *truth,* he is the reality of all God's promises. As the *life,* he joins his divine life to ours, both now and eternally.

14:9 Jesus is the visible, tangible image of the invisible God. He is the complete revelation of what God is like. Jesus explained to Philip, who wanted to see the Father, that to know Jesus is to know God. The search for God, for truth and reality, ends in Christ. (See also Colossians 1:15; Hebrews 1:1–4.)

and the Father is in me; or at least believe on the evidence of the miracles themselves. 12I tell you the truth, anyone who has faith in me will do what I have been
doing. He will do even greater things than these, because I am going to the Father.
13And I will do whatever you ask in my name, so that the Son may bring glory to
the Father. 14You may ask me for anything in my name, and I will do it.

14:12
Acts 5:15
19:11,12

Jesus Promises the Holy Spirit

15"If you love me, you will obey what I command. 16And I will ask the Father,
and he will give you another Counselor to be with you forever— 17the Spirit of
truth. The world cannot accept him, because it neither sees him nor knows him. But
you know him, for he lives with you and will be*ª* in you. 18I will not leave you as
orphans; I will come to you. 19Before long, the world will not see me anymore, but
you will see me. Because I live, you also will live. 20On that day you will realize
that I am in my Father, and you are in me, and I am in you. 21Whoever has my
commands and obeys them, he is the one who loves me. He who loves me will be
loved by my Father, and I too will love him and show myself to him."

22Then Judas (not Judas Iscariot) said, "But, Lord, why do you intend to show
yourself to us and not to the world?"

23Jesus replied, "If anyone loves me, he will obey my teaching. My Father will
love him, and we will come to him and make our home with him. 24He who does
not love me will not obey my teaching. These words you hear are not my own; they
belong to the Father who sent me.

25"All this I have spoken while still with you. 26But the Counselor, the Holy
Spirit, whom the Father will send in my name, will teach you all things and will

14:16
Jn 14:26; 15:26
14:17
Rom 8:15,16
1 Jn 3:24
14:18
Rom 8:9-11
14:20
Jn 10:38; 15:4,5
16:16,23
17:21-24
14:21
Jn 15:10; 16:27
1 Jn 2:5
2 Jn 6
14:22
Lk 6:14-16
Acts 10:40
14:23
Jn 15:10
1 Jn 4:16; 5:3
Rev 3:20; 21:3
14:24
Jn 7:16; 14:10

ª17 Some early manuscripts and is

14:12, 13 Jesus is not saying that his disciples would do more
amazing miracles—after all, raising the dead is about as amazing
as you can get. Rather, the disciples, working in the power of the
Holy Spirit, would carry the gospel of God's kingdom out of Palestine and into the whole world.

14:14 When Jesus says we can ask for anything, we must remember that our asking must be in his name—that is, according to
God's character and will. God will not grant requests contrary to
his nature or his will, and we cannot use his name as a magic formula to fulfill our selfish desires. If we are sincerely following God
and seeking to do his will, then our requests will be in line with
what he wants, and he will grant them. (See also 15:16; 16:23.)

14:15, 16 Jesus was soon going to leave the disciples, but he
would remain with them. How could this be? The Counselor—the
Spirit of God himself—would come after Jesus was gone to care
for and guide the disciples. This happened to the disciples just before his ascension (21:22), and to all the believers at Pentecost
(Acts 2) shortly after Jesus ascended to heaven. The Holy Spirit is
the very presence of God within us and all believers, helping us
live as God wants and building Christ's church on earth. By faith
we can appropriate his power each day.

●**14:16** The word translated *Counselor* combines the ideas of comfort and counsel. The Holy Spirit is a powerful person on our side,
working for and with us.

●**14:17ff** The following chapters teach these truths about the Holy
Spirit: he will never leave us (14:16); the world at large cannot recognize him (14:17); he lives with us and in us (14:17); he teaches
us (14:26); he reminds us of Jesus' words (14:26; 15:26); he convicts us of sin, shows us God's righteousness, and announces
God's judgment on evil (16:8); he guides into truth and gives insight into future events (16:13); he glorifies Christ (16:14). The Holy
Spirit has been active among people from the beginning of time,
but after Pentecost (Acts 2) he came to live in all believers. Many
people are unaware of the Holy Spirit's activities, but to those who
receive Christ's word and understand the Spirit's power, he gives a
whole new way to look at life.

14:18 When Jesus said, "I will come to you," he meant it. Although
Jesus ascended to heaven, he sent the Holy Spirit to live in believers, and to have the Holy Spirit is to have Jesus himself.

14:19–21 Sometimes people wish they knew the future so they
could prepare for it. God has chosen not to give us this knowledge. He alone knows what will happen, but he tells us all we need
to know to *prepare* for the future. When we live by his standards,
he will not leave us, he will come to us, he will be within us, and he
will reveal himself to us. God knows what will happen and, because he will be with us through it, we need not fear. We don't
have to know the future to have faith in God; we have to have faith
in God to be secure about the future.

14:21 Jesus said that his followers show their love by obeying him.
Love is more than lovely words; it is commitment and conduct. If
you love Christ, then prove it by obeying what he says in his Word.

14:22, 23 Because the disciples were still expecting Jesus to establish an earthly kingdom and overthrow Rome, they found it hard
to understand why he did not tell the world at large that he was the
Messiah. Not everyone, however, could understand his message.
Ever since Pentecost, the gospel of the kingdom has been proclaimed in the whole world, and yet not everyone is receptive to it.
Jesus saves the deepest revelations of himself for those who love
and obey him.

14:26 Jesus promised the disciples that the Holy Spirit would help
them remember what he had been teaching them. This promise
ensures the validity of the New Testament. The disciples were eyewitnesses of Jesus' life and teachings, and the Holy Spirit helped
them remember without taking away their individual perspective.
We can be confident that the Gospels are accurate records of
what Jesus taught and did (see 1 Corinthians 2:10–14). The Holy
Spirit can help us in the same way. As we study the Bible, we can
trust him to plant truth in our minds, convince us of God's will, and
remind us when we stray from it.

remind you of everything I have said to you. 27Peace I leave with you; my peace I give you. I do not give to you as the world gives. Do not let your hearts be troubled and do not be afraid.

28"You heard me say, 'I am going away and I am coming back to you.' If you loved me, you would be glad that I am going to the Father, for the Father is greater than I. 29I have told you now before it happens, so that when it does happen you will believe. 30I will not speak with you much longer, for the prince of this world is coming. He has no hold on me, 31but the world must learn that I love the Father and that I do exactly what my Father has commanded me.

"Come now; let us leave.

The Vine and the Branches

15 "I am the true vine, and my Father is the gardener. 2He cuts off every branch in me that bears no fruit, while every branch that does bear fruit he prunes*a* so that it will be even more fruitful. 3You are already clean because of the word I have spoken to you. 4Remain in me, and I will remain in you. No branch can bear fruit by itself; it must remain in the vine. Neither can you bear fruit unless you remain in me.

5"I am the vine; you are the branches. If a man remains in me and I in him, he will bear much fruit; apart from me you can do nothing. 6If anyone does not remain in me, he is like a branch that is thrown away and withers; such branches are picked up, thrown into the fire and burned. 7If you remain in me and my words remain in you, ask whatever you wish, and it will be given you. 8This is to my Father's glory, that you bear much fruit, showing yourselves to be my disciples.

9"As the Father has loved me, so have I loved you. Now remain in my love. 10If

a2 The Greek for prunes also means cleans.

14:26
Lk 24:49
Jn 1:33; 15:26
16:7; 20:22
1 Jn 2:20,27

14:27
Jn 16:33; 20:19

14:29
Jn 13:19

14:30
Jn 12:31

14:31
Jn 10:18; 12:49

15:1
Ps 80:8

15:3
Jn 17:17

15:5
Hos 14:8

15:6
Heb 6:4-6

15:8
Mt 5:15,16

15:9
Jn 3:35
17:23-26

15:10
Jn 8:29

14:27 The result of the Holy Spirit's work in our lives is deep and lasting peace. Unlike worldly peace, which is usually defined as the absence of conflict, this peace is confident assurance in any circumstance; with Christ's peace, we have no need to fear the present or the future. If your life is full of stress, allow the Holy Spirit to fill you with Christ's peace (see Philippians 4:6, 7 for more on experiencing God's peace).

14:27–29 Sin, fear, uncertainty, doubt, and numerous other forces are at war within us. The peace of God moves into our hearts and lives to restrain these hostile forces and offer comfort in place of conflict. Jesus says he will give us that peace if we are willing to accept it from him.

14:28 As God the Son, Jesus willingly submits to God the Father. On earth, Jesus also submitted to many of the physical limitations of being human (Philippians 2:6).

14:30, 31 Although Satan, the prince of this world, was unable to overpower Jesus (Matthew 4), he still had the arrogance to try. Satan's power exists only because God allows him to act. But because Jesus is sinless, Satan has no power over him. If we obey Jesus and align ourselves closely with God's purposes, Satan can have no power over us.

14:31 "Come now; let us leave" suggests that chapters 15—17 may have been spoken en route to the Garden of Gethsemane. Another view is that Jesus was asking the disciples to get ready to leave the upper room, but they did not actually do so until 18:1.

15:1 The grapevine is a prolific plant; a single vine bears many grapes. In the Old Testament, grapes symbolized Israel's fruitfulness in doing God's work on the earth (Psalm 80:8; Isaiah 5:1–7; Ezekiel 19:10–14). In the Passover meal, the fruit of the vine symbolized God's goodness to his people.

●15:1ff Christ is the vine, and God is the gardener who cares for the branches to make them fruitful. The branches are all who claim to be followers of Christ. The fruitful branches are true believers who by their living union with Christ produce much fruit. But those who become unproductive—those who turn back from following Christ after making a superficial commitment—will be separated from the vine. Unproductive followers are as good as dead and will be cut off and cast aside.

●15:2, 3 Jesus makes a distinction between two kinds of pruning: (1) separating and (2) cutting back branches. Fruitful branches are cut back to promote growth. In other words, God must sometimes discipline us to strengthen our character and faith. But branches that don't bear fruit are cut off at the trunk, because not only are they worthless, they often infect the rest of the tree. Those who won't bear fruit for God or who try to block the efforts of God's followers will be cut off from the divine flow of life.

15:5 Fruit is not limited to soul-winning. In this chapter, answered prayer, joy, and love are mentioned as fruit (15:7, 11, 12). Galatians 5:22–24 and 2 Peter 1:5–8 describe additional fruit: qualities of the Christian character like peace and patience.

●15:5, 6 Remaining in Christ means (1) believing he is God's Son (1 John 4:15), (2) receiving him as Savior and Lord (John 1:12), (3) doing what God says (1 John 3:24), (4) continuing in faith (1 John 2:24), and (5) relating to the community of believers, Christ's body (John 15:12).

●15:5-8 Many people try to do good, be honest, and do what is right. But Jesus says the only way to live a truly good life is to stay close to him, like a branch attached to the vine. Apart from him our efforts are unfruitful. Are you receiving the nourishment and life offered by Christ, the vine? If not, you are missing a special gift he has for you.

15:8 When a vine bears "much fruit," God is glorified, for daily he sent the sunshine and rain to make the crops grow, and constantly he nurtured each tiny plant and prepared it to blossom. What a moment of glory for the Lord of the harvest when the harvest is brought into the barns, safe and ready for use! He made it all happen! This farming analogy shows how God is glorified when people come into a right relationship with him and begin to "bear much fruit" in their lives.

15:11
Jn 16:24; 17:13
15:12
1 Jn 3:11
15:13
Jn 10:11

you obey my commands, you will remain in my love, just as I have obeyed my Father's commands and remain in his love. 11I have told you this so that my joy may be in you and that your joy may be complete. 12My command is this: Love each other as I have loved you. 13Greater love has no one than this, that he lay down his life for his friends. 14You are my friends if you do what I command. 15I no longer call you servants, because a servant does not know his master's business. Instead, I have called you friends, for everything that I learned from my Father I have made known to you. 16You did not choose me, but I chose you and appointed you to go and bear fruit—fruit that will last. Then the Father will give you whatever you ask in my name. 17This is my command: Love each other.

15:18
Jn 7:7
1 Jn 3:1,13
15:19
Jn 17:14
1 Jn 4:5,6
15:21
Jn 17:25
15:22
Jn 9:41
15:24
Jn 5:36-38
10:37,38
15:25
Ps 35:19; 69:4
15:26
Jn 14:15-17,26
15:27
Jn 19:35; 21:24
1 Jn 1:1,2

The World Hates the Disciples

18"If the world hates you, keep in mind that it hated me first. 19If you belonged to the world, it would love you as its own. As it is, you do not belong to the world, but I have chosen you out of the world. That is why the world hates you. 20Remember the words I spoke to you: 'No servant is greater than his master.'[a] If they persecuted me, they will persecute you also. If they obeyed my teaching, they will obey yours also. 21They will treat you this way because of my name, for they do not know the One who sent me. 22If I had not come and spoken to them, they would not be guilty of sin. Now, however, they have no excuse for their sin. 23He who hates me hates my Father as well. 24If I had not done among them what no one else did, they would not be guilty of sin. But now they have seen these miracles, and yet they have hated both me and my Father. 25But this is to fulfill what is written in their Law: 'They hated me without reason.'[b]

26"When the Counselor comes, whom I will send to you from the Father, the Spirit of truth who goes out from the Father, he will testify about me. 27And you also must testify, for you have been with me from the beginning.

16:2
Acts 8:1; 9:1
26:9
16:3
Acts 3:17

16 "All this I have told you so that you will not go astray. 2They will put you out of the synagogue; in fact, a time is coming when anyone who kills you will think he is offering a service to God. 3They will do such things because they have not known the Father or me. 4I have told you this, so that when the time comes you

a20 John 13:16   *b25* Psalms 35:19; 69:4

15:11 When things are going well, we feel elated. When hardships come, we sink into depression. But true joy transcends these waves of circumstance. Joy comes from a consistent relationship with Jesus Christ. When our lives are intertwined with his, he will help us walk through adversity without sinking into debilitating lows and manage prosperity without moving into deceptive highs. The joy of living with Jesus Christ daily keeps us levelheaded no matter how high or low our circumstances.

15:12, 13 We are to love each other as Jesus loved us, and he loved us enough to give his life for us. We may not have to die for someone, but there are other ways to practice sacrificial love: listening, helping, encouraging, giving. Think of someone in particular who needs this kind of love today. Give all the love you can, and then try to give a little more.

15:15 Because Jesus Christ is Lord and Master, he should call us slaves, but instead he calls us friends. How comforting and reassuring to be chosen as his friends. Because he is Lord and Master, our obedience should be unqualified and blind, but Jesus asks us to obey him because we love him.

15:16 Jesus made the first choice—to love and to die for us, to invite us to live with him forever. We make the next choice—to accept or reject his offer. Without *his* choice, we would have no choice to make.

15:17 Christians will get plenty of hatred from the world; from each other we need love and support. Do you allow small problems to

get in the way of loving other believers? Jesus commands that you love them, and he will give you the strength to do it.

15:26 Once again Jesus offers hope. The Holy Spirit gives strength to endure the unreasonable hatred and evil in our world and the hostility many have toward Christ. This is especially comforting for those facing persecution.

15:26 Jesus uses two names for the Holy Spirit—*Counselor* and *Spirit of truth*. The word *Counselor* conveys the helping, encouraging, and strengthening work of the Spirit. *Spirit of truth* points to the teaching, illuminating, and reminding work of the Spirit. The Holy Spirit ministers to both the head and the heart, and both dimensions are important.

16:1–16 In his last moments with his disciples, Jesus (1) warned them about further persecution, (2) told them where, when, and why he was going, and (3) assured them they would not be left alone, but that the Spirit would come. He knew what lay ahead, and he did not want their faith shaken or destroyed. God wants you to know you are not alone. You have the Holy Spirit to comfort you, teach you truth, and help you.

16:2 A vivid fulfillment of this prediction happened when Stephen was expelled from the synagogue and stoned to death (Acts 7:57–60). Saul (who later became Paul), under the authority of the high priest, went through the land hunting down and persecuting Christians (Acts 9:1, 2).

will remember that I warned you. I did not tell you this at first because I was with you.

16:4
Jn 13:19; 14:29

The Work of the Holy Spirit

5"Now I am going to him who sent me, yet none of you asks me, 'Where are you going?' 6Because I have said these things, you are filled with grief. 7But I tell you the truth: It is for your good that I am going away. Unless I go away, the Counselor will not come to you; but if I go, I will send him to you. 8When he comes, he will convict the world of guilt*a* in regard to sin and righteousness and judgment: 9in regard to sin, because men do not believe in me; 10in regard to righteousness, because I am going to the Father, where you can see me no longer; 11and in regard to judgment, because the prince of this world now stands condemned.

16:5
Jn 7:33; 13:36

16:9
Rom 1:18-23
3:9,10; 14:23

16:10
Acts 3:14; 7:52

16:11
Lk 10:18
Jn 12:31
Heb 2:14

12"I have much more to say to you, more than you can now bear. 13But when he, the Spirit of truth, comes, he will guide you into all truth. He will not speak on his own; he will speak only what he hears, and he will tell you what is yet to come. 14He will bring glory to me by taking from what is mine and making it known to you. 15All that belongs to the Father is mine. That is why I said the Spirit will take from what is mine and make it known to you.

16:13
Jn 14:26

16:15
Mt 11:27
Jn 17:10
Col 2:9,10

16"In a little while you will see me no more, and then after a little while you will see me."

16:16
Jn 14:3,19-25

The Disciples' Grief Will Turn to Joy

17Some of his disciples said to one another, "What does he mean by saying, 'In a little while you will see me no more, and then after a little while you will see me,' and 'Because I am going to the Father'?" 18They kept asking, "What does he mean by 'a little while'? We don't understand what he is saying."

19Jesus saw that they wanted to ask him about this, so he said to them, "Are you asking one another what I meant when I said, 'In a little while you will see me no more, and then after a little while you will see me'? 20I tell you the truth, you will weep and mourn while the world rejoices. You will grieve, but your grief will turn to joy. 21A woman giving birth to a child has pain because her time has come; but when her baby is born she forgets the anguish because of her joy that a child is born into the world. 22So with you: Now is your time of grief, but I will see you again and you will rejoice, and no one will take away your joy. 23In that day you will no longer ask me anything. I tell you the truth, my Father will give you whatever you

16:20
Mk 16:10
Lk 23:27
Jn 20:19,20

16:21
Isa 26:16-19
Acts 13:33
Col 1:18

16:22
Jn 20:19,20

16:23
Jn 14:20
15:16; 16:26

a8 Or will expose the guilt of the world

16:5 Although the disciples had asked Jesus about his death (13:36; 14:5), they had never wondered about its meaning. They were mostly concerned about themselves. If Jesus went, what would become of them?

16:7 Unless Jesus did what he came to do, there would be no gospel. If he did not die, he could not remove our sins; he could not rise again and defeat death. If he did not go back to the Father, the Holy Spirit would not come. Christ's presence on earth was limited to one place at a time. His leaving meant he could be present to the whole world through the Holy Spirit.

16:8–11 Three important tasks of the Holy Spirit are (1) convincing the world of its sin and calling it to repentance, (2) showing the standard of God's righteousness to anyone who believes because Christ would no longer be physically present on earth, and (3) demonstrating Christ's judgment over Satan.

16:9 According to Jesus, unbelief in him is *sin.*

16:10, 11 Christ's death on the cross made a personal relationship with God available to us. When we confess our sin, God declares us righteous and delivers us from judgment for our sins.

16:13 The truth into which the Holy Spirit guides us is the truth about Christ. He also helps us through patient practice to discern right from wrong.

16:13 Jesus said the Holy Spirit would show them "what is yet to

come"—the nature of their mission, the opposition they would face, and the final outcome of their efforts. They didn't fully understand these promises until the Holy Spirit came after Jesus' death and resurrection. Then the Holy Spirit revealed truths to the disciples that they wrote down in the books that now form the New Testament.

16:16 Jesus was referring to his death, now only a few hours away, and his resurrection three days later.

16:20 What a contrast between the disciples and the world! The world rejoiced as the disciples wept, but they would see him again (in three days) and rejoice. The world's values are often the opposite of God's values. This can cause Christians to feel like misfits. But even if life is difficult now, one day we will rejoice. Keep your eye on the future and on God's promises!

16:23–27 Jesus is talking about a new relationship between the believer and God. Previously, people approached God through priests. After Jesus' resurrection, any believer could approach God directly. A new day has dawned and now all believers are priests, talking with God personally and directly (see Hebrews 10:19–23). We approach God, not because of our own merit, but because Jesus, our great high priest, has made us acceptable to God.

16:30 The disciples believed Jesus' words because they were convinced he knew everything. But their belief was only a first step

16:24
Jn 15:11

16:25
Jn 10:6; 16:29

16:27
Jn 8:42; 14:21
17:8

16:28
Jn 1:14
6:32,46
8:42; 13:1,3
17:11,13

16:32
Zech 13:7
Mt 26:31
Jn 8:29

16:33
Jn 14:27
Eph 2:14
Col 1:20

ask in my name. 24Until now you have not asked for anything in my name. Ask and you will receive, and your joy will be complete.

25"Though I have been speaking figuratively, a time is coming when I will no longer use this kind of language but will tell you plainly about my Father. 26In that day you will ask in my name. I am not saying that I will ask the Father on your behalf. 27No, the Father himself loves you because you have loved me and have believed that I came from God. 28I came from the Father and entered the world; now I am leaving the world and going back to the Father."

29Then Jesus' disciples said, "Now you are speaking clearly and without figures of speech. 30Now we can see that you know all things and that you do not even need to have anyone ask you questions. This makes us believe that you came from God."

31"You believe at last!"*a* Jesus answered. 32"But a time is coming, and has come, when you will be scattered, each to his own home. You will leave me all alone. Yet I am not alone, for my Father is with me.

33"I have told you these things, so that in me you may have peace. In this world you will have trouble. But take heart! I have overcome the world."

Jesus Prays for Himself

17:1
Jn 7:39
13:31,32

17:2
Jn 3:35; 6:37

17:3
Phil 3:8,10
1 Jn 5:20

17:5
Jn 1:1,2; 17:24
Phil 2:6

17 After Jesus said this, he looked toward heaven and prayed:

"Father, the time has come. Glorify your Son, that your Son may glorify you. 2For you granted him authority over all people that he might give eternal life to all those you have given him. 3Now this is eternal life: that they may know you, the only true God, and Jesus Christ, whom you have sent. 4I have brought you glory on earth by completing the work you gave me to do. 5And now, Father, glorify me in your presence with the glory I had with you before the world began.

Jesus Prays for His Disciples

17:6
Jn 17:26

17:8
Jn 15:15; 16:50

17:9
1 Jn 5:19

17:10
Rom 8:29,30
Eph 3:21

6"I have revealed you*b* to those whom you gave me out of the world. They were yours; you gave them to me and they have obeyed your word. 7Now they know that everything you have given me comes from you. 8For I gave them the words you gave me and they accepted them. They knew with certainty that I came from you, and they believed that you sent me. 9I pray for them. I am not praying for the world, but for those you have given me, for they are yours. 10All I have is yours, and all you have is mine. And glory has come to me through them. 11I will remain in the world no longer, but they are still in the

a31 Or "Do you now believe?"   b6 Greek your name; also in verse 26

---

toward the great faith they would receive when the Holy Spirit came to indwell them.

16:31–33 As Christians, we should expect continuing tension with an unbelieving world that is "out of sync" with Christ, his gospel, and his people. At the same time, we can expect our relationship with Christ to produce peace and comfort, because we are "in sync" with him.

16:32 The disciples scattered after Jesus was arrested (see Mark 14:50).

16:33 Jesus sums up all he has told them this night, tying together themes from 14:27–29; 16:1–4; and 16:9–11. With these words he tells his disciples to take courage. In spite of the inevitable struggles they will face, they are not alone. Jesus does not abandon us to our struggles either. If we remember that the ultimate victory has already been won, we can claim the peace of Christ in the most troublesome times.

●**17:1ff** This entire chapter is Jesus' prayer. From it we learn that the world is a tremendous battleground where the forces under Satan's power and those under God's authority are at war. Satan and his forces are motivated by bitter hatred for Christ and his forces. Jesus prayed for his disciples, including those of us who follow him today. He prayed that God would keep his chosen believers safe

from Satan's power, making them pure and holy, uniting them through his truth.

17:3 How do we get eternal life? Jesus tells us clearly here—by knowing God the Father himself through his Son, Jesus Christ. Eternal life requires entering into a personal relationship with God in Jesus Christ. When we admit our sin and turn away from it, Christ's love lives in us by the Holy Spirit.

17:5 Before Jesus came to earth, he was one with God. Now that his mission on earth was almost finished, he was asking his Father to restore him to his original place of honor and authority. Jesus' resurrection and ascension—and Stephen's dying exclamation (Acts 7:56)—attest that Jesus did return to his exalted position at the right hand of God.

17:10 What did Jesus mean when he said "glory has come to me through them"? God's glory is the revelation of his character and presence. The lives of Jesus' disciples reveal his character, and he is present to the world through them. Does your life reveal Jesus' character and presence?

●**17:11** Jesus is asking that the disciples be united in harmony and love as the Father, Son, and Holy Spirit are united—the strongest of all unions. (See the note on 17:21–23.)

world, and I am coming to you. Holy Father, protect them by the power of your name—the name you gave me—so that they may be one as we are one. 12While I was with them, I protected them and kept them safe by that name you gave me. None has been lost except the one doomed to destruction so that Scripture would be fulfilled.

13"I am coming to you now, but I say these things while I am still in the world, so that they may have the full measure of my joy within them. 14I have given them your word and the world has hated them, for they are not of the world any more than I am of the world. 15My prayer is not that you take them out of the world but that you protect them from the evil one. 16They are not of the world, even as I am not of it. 17Sanctify*a* them by the truth; your word is truth. 18As you sent me into the world, I have sent them into the world. 19For them I sanctify myself, that they too may be truly sanctified.

Jesus Prays for All Believers

20"My prayer is not for them alone. I pray also for those who will believe in me through their message, 21that all of them may be one, Father, just as you are in me and I am in you. May they also be in us so that the world may believe that you have sent me. 22I have given them the glory that you gave me, that they may be one as we are one: 23I in them and you in me. May they be brought to complete unity to let the world know that you sent me and have loved them even as you have loved me.

24"Father, I want those you have given me to be with me where I am, and to see my glory, the glory you have given me because you loved me before the creation of the world.

25"Righteous Father, though the world does not know you, I know you, and they know that you have sent me. 26I have made you known to them, and will continue to make you known in order that the love you have for me may be in them and that I myself may be in them."

2. Jesus Completes His Mission
Jesus Arrested

18 When he had finished praying, Jesus left with his disciples and crossed the Kidron Valley. On the other side there was an olive grove, and he and his disciples went into it.

2Now Judas, who betrayed him, knew the place, because Jesus had often met there with his disciples. 3So Judas came to the grove, guiding a detachment of

a17 Greek hagiazo (set apart for sacred use or make holy); also in verse 19

Side references:

17:11 Jn 10:30; 17:21 Gal 3:28
17:12 Jn 6:39; 10:28 Acts 1:20 Heb 2:13 1 Jn 2:19
17:13 Jn 7:33; 15:11
17:14 Jn 15:19
17:15 1 Jn 5:18
17:18 Jn 20:21
17:19 Heb 2:11
17:20 Acts 2:40,41 4:29,31; 10:44
17:21 Jn 10:30,38 14:11; 17:11 Eph 4:3-6
17:22 2 Cor 4:6 Eph 3:16,21
17:23 Jn 10:38 16:27; 17:11
17:24 Jn 1:14; 12:26
17:26 Jn 15:9
18:1 2 Sam 15:23 2 Kgs 23:4,6,12 2 Chron 15:16 29:16; 30:14

17:12 Judas was the "one doomed to destruction" who perished because he betrayed Jesus (see Psalm 41:9).

17:13 Joy is a common theme in Christ's teachings—he wants us to be joyful (see 15:11; 16:24, 33). The key to immeasurable joy is living in close contact with him, the source of all joy. When we do we will experience God's special care and protection and see the victory God brings even when defeat seems certain.

17:14 The world hates Christians because Christians' values differ from the world's. Since Christ's followers don't cooperate with the world by joining in their sin, they are living accusations against the world's immorality. The world follows Satan's agenda, and Satan is the avowed enemy of Jesus and his people.

17:17 A follower of Christ becomes sanctified (set apart for sacred use, cleansed and made holy) through believing and obeying the Word of God (Hebrews 4:12). He or she has already accepted forgiveness through Christ's sacrificial death (Hebrews 7:26, 27). But daily application of God's Word has a purifying effect on our minds and hearts. It points out sin, motivates us to confess, renews our relationship with Christ, and guides us back to the right path.

17:18 Jesus didn't ask God to take believers *out* of the world but instead to use them *in* the world. Because Jesus sends us into the world, we should not try to escape from the world or avoid all relationships with non-Christians. We are called to be salt and light (Matthew 5:13–16), and we are to do the work God sent us to do.

●**17:20** Jesus prayed for all who would follow him, including you and others you know. He prayed for oneness (17:11), protection from the evil one (17:15), and sanctity (holiness) (17:17). Knowing that Jesus prayed for us should give us confidence as we work for his kingdom.

17:21–23 Jesus' great desire for his disciples was that they become one. He wanted them unified as a powerful witness to the reality of God's love. Are you helping to unify the body of Christ, the church? You can pray for other Christians, avoid gossip, build others up, work together in humility, give your time and money, lift up Christ, and refuse to get sidetracked arguing over divisive matters.

17:21–23 Jesus prayed for unity among the believers based on the believers' oneness with him and the Father. Christians can know unity among themselves if they are living in union with God. For example, each branch living in union with the vine is united with all other branches doing the same.

18:3 The soldiers were members of the temple guard; they were Jews given authority by the religious leaders to make arrests for

soldiers and some officials from the chief priests and Pharisees. They were carrying torches, lanterns and weapons.

4Jesus, knowing all that was going to happen to him, went out and asked them, "Who is it you want?"

5"Jesus of Nazareth," they replied.

"I am he," Jesus said. (And Judas the traitor was standing there with them.) 6When Jesus said, "I am he," they drew back and fell to the ground.

7Again he asked them, "Who is it you want?"

And they said, "Jesus of Nazareth."

18:9
Jn 17:12

8"I told you that I am he," Jesus answered. "If you are looking for me, then let these men go." 9This happened so that the words he had spoken would be fulfilled: "I have not lost one of those you gave me."*a*

18:10
Mt 26:51
Mk 14:47
Lk 22:49,50

10Then Simon Peter, who had a sword, drew it and struck the high priest's servant, cutting off his right ear. (The servant's name was Malchus.)

18:11
Mt 20:22
26:39,42

11Jesus commanded Peter, "Put your sword away! Shall I not drink the cup the Father has given me?"

Jesus Taken to Annas

18:12
Mt 26:57

12Then the detachment of soldiers with its commander and the Jewish officials arrested Jesus. They bound him 13and brought him first to Annas, who was the

*a*9 John 6:39

---

minor infractions. The detachment of men may have been a small contingent of Roman soldiers who did not participate in the arrest but accompanied the temple officers to make sure matters didn't get out of control.

18:4, 5 John does not record Judas's kiss of greeting (Matthew 26:49; Mark 14:45; Luke 22:47, 48); but his kiss marked a turning point for the disciples, because with Jesus' arrest each one's life would be radically different. For the first time, Judas openly betrayed Jesus before the other disciples. For the first time, Jesus' loyal disciples ran away from him (Matthew 26:56). The band of disciples would undergo severe testing before they were transformed from uncertain followers to dynamic leaders.

18:6 The men may have been startled by Jesus' statement or by the words "I am he," a declaration of his divinity (Exodus 3:14). Or perhaps they were overcome by his obvious power and authority.

●**18:10, 11** Trying to protect Jesus, Peter pulled a sword and wounded the high priest's servant. But Jesus told him to put away his sword and allow God's plan to unfold. At times it is tempting to take matters into our own hands, to force the issue. Most often such moves lead to sin. Instead we must trust God to work out his plan. Think of it—if Peter had had his way, Jesus would not have gone to the cross, and God's plan of redemption would have been halted.

●**18:11** The cup means the suffering, isolation, and death that Jesus would have to endure in order to atone for the sins of the world.

18:12, 13 Jesus was immediately taken to the high priest's residence, even though this was the middle of the night. The religious leaders were in a hurry—they wanted to complete the execution before the Sabbath and get on with the Passover celebration. This residence was a palace whose outer walls enclosed a courtyard where servants and soldiers warmed themselves around a fire.

●**18:13** Both Annas and Caiaphas are called high priests. Annas was Israel's high priest from A.D. 6 to 15, when he was deposed by Roman rulers. Caiaphas, Annas's son-in-law, was appointed high priest from A.D. 18 to 36/37. According to Jewish law, the office of high priest was held for life. Many Jews therefore still considered Annas the high priest and still called him by that title. But although Annas retained much authority among the Jews, Caiaphas made the final decisions.

Both Caiaphas and Annas cared more about their political ambitions than about their responsibility to lead the people to God.

Though religious leaders, they had become evil. As the nation's spiritual leaders, they should have been sensitive to God's revelation in his Word. They should have known that Jesus was the Messiah about whom the Scriptures spoke, and they should have pointed the people to him. But when men pursue evil, they want to eliminate all opposition. Instead of honestly evaluating Jesus' claims based on their knowledge of Scripture, they sought to further their own selfish ambitions, killing God's Son to do it.

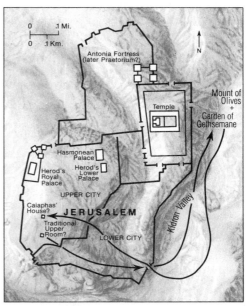

BETRAYAL IN THE GARDEN After eating the Passover meal in the upper room, Jesus and his disciples went to Gethsemane, where Judas led the temple guard to arrest Jesus. Jesus was then taken to Caiaphas's house for his first of many trials.

father-in-law of Caiaphas, the high priest that year. ¹⁴Caiaphas was the one who
had advised the Jews that it would be good if one man died for the people.

18:14
Jn 11:50

Peter's First Denial

¹⁵Simon Peter and another disciple were following Jesus. Because this disciple
was known to the high priest, he went with Jesus into the high priest's courtyard,
¹⁶but Peter had to wait outside at the door. The other disciple, who was known to
the high priest, came back, spoke to the girl on duty there and brought Peter in.

18:15
Mt 26:58
Lk 22:54
18:16
Mt 26:69

¹⁷"You are not one of his disciples, are you?" the girl at the door asked Peter.
He replied, "I am not."

¹⁸It was cold, and the servants and officials stood around a fire they had made to
keep warm. Peter also was standing with them, warming himself.

18:18
Mk 14:54

The High Priest Questions Jesus

¹⁹Meanwhile, the high priest questioned Jesus about his disciples and his teaching.

18:19
Mt 26:59-68
Mk 14:55-65
Lk 22:63-71

²⁰"I have spoken openly to the world," Jesus replied. "I always taught in syna-
gogues or at the temple, where all the Jews come together. I said nothing in secret.
²¹Why question me? Ask those who heard me. Surely they know what I said."

18:20
Mt 26:55
Lk 4:15
Jn 7:14,26,28

²²When Jesus said this, one of the officials nearby struck him in the face. "Is this
the way you answer the high priest?" he demanded.

18:22
Isa 50:6
Jn 19:3

²³"If I said something wrong," Jesus replied, "testify as to what is wrong. But if
I spoke the truth, why did you strike me?" ²⁴Then Annas sent him, still bound, to
Caiaphas the high priest. ᵃ

18:23
Mt 5:39
Acts 23:2

Peter's Second and Third Denials

²⁵As Simon Peter stood warming himself, he was asked, "You are not one of his
disciples, are you?"

18:25
Mt 26:73-75

He denied it, saying, "I am not."

²⁶One of the high priest's servants, a relative of the man whose ear Peter had cut
off, challenged him, "Didn't I see you with him in the olive grove?" ²⁷Again Peter
denied it, and at that moment a rooster began to crow.

18:27
Jn 13:38

Jesus before Pilate

²⁸Then the Jews led Jesus from Caiaphas to the palace of the Roman governor.
By now it was early morning, and to avoid ceremonial uncleanness the Jews did not

18:28
Mt 27:2

ᵃ24 Or (Now Annas had sent him, still bound, to Caiaphas the high priest.)

18:15, 16 The other disciple is John, the author of this Gospel. He knew the high priest and identified himself to the girl at the gate. Because of his connections, he got himself and Peter into the courtyard. But Peter refused to identify himself as Jesus' follower. Peter's experiences in the next few hours would change his life. For more information about Peter, see his Profile in Matthew 26.

18:19ff During the night, Jesus had two pre-trial hearings before he was taken before the entire Jewish council (18:24 mentions the second pre-trial hearing). The religious leaders knew they had no grounds for charging him, so they tried to build evidence against him by using false witnesses.

●**18:22–27** We can easily get angry at the Jewish council for their injustice in condemning Jesus, but we must remember that Peter and the rest of the disciples also contributed to Jesus' pain by deserting and denying him (Matthew 25:56). While most of us are not like the religious leaders, we are all like the disciples, for all of us have been guilty of denying Christ as Lord in vital areas of our lives or of keeping secret our identity as believers in times of pressure. Don't excuse yourself by pointing at others whose sins seem worse than yours. Instead, come to Jesus for forgiveness and healing.

18:25 The other three Gospels say that Peter's three denials hap-

pened near a fire outside Caiaphas's palace. John places the first denial outside Annas's home, the other two outside Caiaphas's home. This was no doubt the same courtyard. The high priest's residence was large, and Annas and Caiaphas lived near each other.

18:25–27 Imagine standing outside while Jesus, your Lord and Master, is questioned. Imagine watching this man, whom you have come to believe is the long-awaited Messiah, being abused and beaten. Naturally Peter was confused and afraid. It is a serious sin to deny Christ, but Jesus forgave Peter (21:15–17). No sin is too great for Jesus to forgive if you are truly repentant. He will forgive even your worst sin if you turn from it and ask his pardon.

18:27 This fulfilled Jesus' words to Peter after he promised he would never deny him (13:38).

18:28 By Jewish law, entering the house of a Gentile would cause a Jewish person to be ceremonially defiled. As a result, he could not take part in worship at the temple or celebrate the feasts until he was restored to a state of "cleanness." Afraid of being defiled, these men stayed outside the house where they had taken Jesus for trial. They kept up the ceremonial requirements of their religion while harboring murder and treachery in their hearts.

enter the palace; they wanted to be able to eat the Passover. 29So Pilate came out to them and asked, "What charges are you bringing against this man?"

30"If he were not a criminal," they replied, "we would not have handed him over to you."

31Pilate said, "Take him yourselves and judge him by your own law."

18:32
Mt 20:19
Jn 12:32,33

"But we have no right to execute anyone," the Jews objected. 32This happened so that the words Jesus had spoken indicating the kind of death he was going to die would be fulfilled.

THE SIX STAGES OF JESUS' TRIAL Although Jesus' trial lasted less than 18 hours, he was taken to six different hearings.	BEFORE JEWISH AUTHORITIES	Preliminary Hearing before Annas (John 18:12–24)	Because the office of high priest was for life, Annas was still the "official" high priest in the eyes of the Jews, even though the Romans had appointed another. Thus Annas still carried much weight among the Sanhedrin.
		Hearing before Caiaphas (Matthew 26:57–68)	Like the hearing before Annas, this hearing was conducted at night in secrecy. It was full of illegalities that made a mockery of justice (see the chart in Matthew 28).
		Trial before the Sanhedrin (Matthew 27:1, 2)	Just after daybreak, 70 members of the Jewish Sanhedrin met to rubber-stamp their approval of the previous hearings to make them appear legal. The purpose of this trial was not to determine justice, but to justify their own preconceptions of Jesus' guilt.
	BEFORE ROMAN AUTHORITIES	First Hearing before Pilate (Luke 23:1–5)	The religious leaders had condemned Jesus to death on religious grounds, but only the Roman government could grant the death penalty. Thus, they took Jesus to Pilate, the Roman governor, and accused him of treason and rebellion, crimes for which the Roman government gave the death penalty. Pilate saw at once that Jesus was innocent, but he was afraid about the uproar being caused by the religious leaders.
		Hearing before Herod (Luke 23:6–12)	Since Jesus' home was in the region of Galilee, Pilate sent Jesus to Herod Agrippa, the ruler of Galilee, who was in Jerusalem for the Passover celebration. Herod was eager to see Jesus do a miracle, but when Jesus remained silent, Herod wanted nothing to do with him and sent him back to Pilate.
		Last Hearing before Pilate (Luke 23:13–25)	Pilate didn't like the religious leaders. He wasn't interested in condemning Jesus because he knew Jesus was innocent. However, he knew that another uprising in his district might cost him his job. First he tried to compromise with the religious leaders by having Jesus beaten, an illegal action in itself. But finally he gave in and handed Jesus over to be executed. His self-interest was stronger than his sense of justice.

18:29 This Roman governor, Pilate, was in charge of Judea (the region where Jerusalem was located) from A.D. 26 to 36. Pilate was unpopular with the Jews because he had raided the temple treasuries for money to build an aqueduct. He did not like the Jews, but when Jesus, the King of the Jews, stood before him, Pilate found him innocent.

18:30 Pilate knew what was going on; he knew that the religious leaders hated Jesus, and he did not want to act as their executioner. They could not sentence him to death themselves—permission had to come from a Roman leader. But Pilate initially refused to sentence Jesus without sufficient evidence. Jesus' life became a pawn in a political power struggle.

●**18:31ff** Pilate made four attempts to deal with Jesus: (1) he tried to put the responsibility on someone else (18:31); (2) he tried to find a way of escape so he could release Jesus (18:39); (3) he tried to compromise with the people—beating Jesus rather than handing him over to die (19:1–3); and (4) he tried a direct appeal to the sympathy of the accusers (19:15). Everyone has to decide what to do with Jesus. Pilate tried to let everyone else decide for him—and in the end, he lost.

18:32 This prediction is recorded in Matthew 20:19. Crucifixion was a common method of execution for criminals who were not Roman citizens.

³³Pilate then went back inside the palace, summoned Jesus and asked him, "Are you the king of the Jews?"

18:33
Lk 23:3
Jn 19:12

³⁴"Is that your own idea," Jesus asked, "or did others talk to you about me?"

³⁵"Am I a Jew?" Pilate replied. "It was your people and your chief priests who handed you over to me. What is it you have done?"

³⁶Jesus said, "My kingdom is not of this world. If it were, my servants would fight to prevent my arrest by the Jews. But now my kingdom is from another place."

18:36
Isa 9:6
Dan 2:44; 7:14
Mt 26:53
Lk 17:20,21
Jn 6:15

³⁷"You are a king, then!" said Pilate.

Jesus answered, "You are right in saying I am a king. In fact, for this reason I was born, and for this I came into the world, to testify to the truth. Everyone on the side of truth listens to me."

18:37
Jn 8:47
1 Jn 3:19; 4:6
Rev 1:5

³⁸"What is truth?" Pilate asked. With this he went out again to the Jews and said, "I find no basis for a charge against him. ³⁹But it is your custom for me to release to you one prisoner at the time of the Passover. Do you want me to release 'the king of the Jews'?"

18:38
Jn 19:4,6
18:39
Mt 27:15-18,
20-23
Mk 15:6-15

⁴⁰They shouted back, "No, not him! Give us Barabbas!" Now Barabbas had taken part in a rebellion.

18:40
Lk 23:17-19

Jesus Sentenced to be Crucified

19 Then Pilate took Jesus and had him flogged. ²The soldiers twisted together a crown of thorns and put it on his head. They clothed him in a purple robe ³and went up to him again and again, saying, "Hail, king of the Jews!" And they struck him in the face.

19:1
Isa 50:6
Mt 27:26-30
Mk 15:15-19
Lk 18:32,33

⁴Once more Pilate came out and said to the Jews, "Look, I am bringing him out to you to let you know that I find no basis for a charge against him." ⁵When Jesus came out wearing the crown of thorns and the purple robe, Pilate said to them, "Here is the man!"

19:3
Jn 18:22
19:4
Jn 18:38
2 Cor 5:21

⁶As soon as the chief priests and their officials saw him, they shouted, "Crucify! Crucify!"

19:6
Acts 3:13

But Pilate answered, "You take him and crucify him. As for me, I find no basis for a charge against him."

⁷The Jews insisted, "We have a law, and according to that law he must die, because he claimed to be the Son of God."

19:7
Lev 24:15,16
Mt 26:63-66

18:34 If Pilate was asking as the Roman governor, he would be inquiring whether Jesus was setting up a rebel government. But the Jews were using the word *king* to mean their religious ruler, the Messiah. Israel was a captive nation, under the authority of the Roman empire. A rival king might have threatened Rome; a Messiah could have been a purely religious leader.

●**18:36, 37** Pilate asked Jesus a straightforward question and Jesus answered clearly. He is a king, but one whose kingdom is not of this world. There seems to have been no question in Pilate's mind that Jesus spoke the truth and was innocent of any crime. It also seems apparent that while recognizing the truth, Pilate chose to reject it, losing the greatest opportunity he would ever have. It is a tragedy when we fail to recognize the truth. It is a greater tragedy when we recognize the truth but fail to heed it.

18:38 Pilate was cynical; he thought all truth was relative. To many government officials, truth was whatever the majority of people agreed with or whatever helped their own personal power and political advancement. When there is no basis for truth, there is no basis for moral right and wrong. Justice becomes whatever works or helps those in power. In Jesus and his Word we have a standard for truth and for our moral behavior.

18:40 Barabbas was a rebel against Rome and, although he had committed murder, was probably a hero among the Jews. The Jews hated being governed by Rome and paying taxes to the despised government. And the Jews hatred of Jesus blinded their

moral reasoning. Barabbas, who had led a rebellion and failed, was released instead of Jesus, the only one who could truly help Israel. For more on Barabbas, see the note on Luke 23:17–19.

19:1ff To grasp the full picture of Jesus' crucifixion, read John's perspective along with the other three accounts in Matthew 27, Mark 15, and Luke 23. Each writer adds meaningful details, but each has the same message—Jesus died on the cross, in fulfillment of Old Testament prophecy, so that we could be saved from our sins and given eternal life.

19:1–3 Flogging could have killed Jesus. The usual procedure was to bare the upper half of the victim's body and tie his hands to a pillar before whipping him with a three-pronged whip. The number of lashes was determined by the severity of the crime; up to 40 were permitted under Jewish law (Deuteronomy 25:3). After being flogged, Jesus also endured other agonies recorded here and in the other Gospels.

19:2–5 The soldiers went beyond their orders to whip Jesus—they also mocked his claim to royalty by placing a crown on his head and a royal robe on his shoulders.

19:7 The truth finally came out—the religious leaders had not brought Jesus to Pilate because he was causing rebellion against Rome, but because they thought he had broken their religious laws. Blasphemy, one of the most serious crimes in Jewish law, deserved the death penalty. Accusing Jesus of blasphemy would give credibility to their case in the eyes of Jews; accusing Jesus of

19:9
Isa 53:7
Mt 27:12,14
Acts 8:32

8When Pilate heard this, he was even more afraid, 9and he went back inside the palace. "Where do you come from?" he asked Jesus, but Jesus gave him no answer. 10"Do you refuse to speak to me?" Pilate said. "Don't you realize I have power either to free you or to crucify you?"

19:11
Acts 2:23; 3:13
Rom 13:1

11Jesus answered, "You would have no power over me if it were not given to you from above. Therefore the one who handed me over to you is guilty of a greater sin."

19:12
Lk 23:2
Acts 17:7

12From then on, Pilate tried to set Jesus free, but the Jews kept shouting, "If you let this man go, you are no friend of Caesar. Anyone who claims to be a king opposes Caesar."

19:13
Mt 27:19

13When Pilate heard this, he brought Jesus out and sat down on the judge's seat at a place known as the Stone Pavement (which in Aramaic is Gabbatha). 14It was the day of Preparation of Passover Week, about the sixth hour.

"Here is your king," Pilate said to the Jews.

15But they shouted, "Take him away! Take him away! Crucify him!"

"Shall I crucify your king?" Pilate asked.

19:16
Mt 27:26,31
Mk 15:15
Lk 23:24

"We have no king but Caesar," the chief priests answered.

16Finally Pilate handed him over to them to be crucified.

The Crucifixion

So the soldiers took charge of Jesus. 17Carrying his own cross, he went out to the

---

treason would give credibility to their case in the eyes of the Romans. They didn't care which accusation Pilate listened to as long as he would cooperate with them in killing Jesus.

●**19:10** Throughout the trial we see that Jesus was in control, not Pilate or the religious leaders. Pilate vacillated, the Jewish leaders reacted out of hatred and anger, but Jesus remained composed. He knew the truth, he knew God's plan, and he knew the reason for his trial. Despite the pressure and persecution, Jesus remained unmoved. It was really Pilate and the religious leaders who were on trial, not Jesus. When you are questioned or ridiculed because of your faith, remember that while you may be on trial before your accusers, they are on trial before God.

19:11 When Jesus said the man who delivered him to Pilate was guiltier than Pilate, he was not excusing Pilate for reacting to the political pressure placed on him. Pilate was responsible for his decision about Jesus. The religious leaders were more guilty because they premeditated Jesus' murder.

19:12, 13 These words pressured Pilate into allowing Jesus to be crucified. As Roman governor of the area, Pilate was expected to keep the peace. Because Rome could not afford to keep large numbers of troops in the outlying regions, they maintained control by crushing rebellions immediately with brute force. Pilate was afraid that reports to Caesar of insurrection in his region would cost him his job and perhaps even his life. When we face a tough decision, we can take the easy way out, or we can stand for what is right regardless of the cost. If we know what is right and don't do it, we sin (James 4:17).

19:13 The Stone Pavement was part of the Tower of Antonia bordering the northwest corner of the temple complex.

19:15 The Jewish leaders were so desperate to get rid of Jesus that, despite their intense hatred for Rome, they shouted, "We have no king but Caesar." How ironic that they feigned allegiance to Rome while rejecting their own Messiah! Their own words condemned them, for God was to be their only true King and they had abandoned every trace of loyalty to him. The priests had truly lost their reason for being—instead of turning people to God, they claimed allegiance to Rome in order to kill their Messiah.

19:17 This place called *Golgotha,* "the skull," was probably a hill

outside Jerusalem along a main road. Many executions took place here so the Romans could use them as an example to the people.

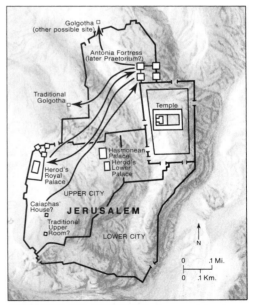

JESUS' TRIAL AND CRUCIFIXION   Jesus was taken from trial before the Jewish Sanhedrin to trial before the Roman procurator, Pilate, in the Antonia Fortress. Pilate sent him to Herod (Luke 23:5–12), but Herod just returned Jesus to Pilate. Responding to threats from the mob, Pilate finally turned Jesus over to be crucified.

place of the Skull (which in Aramaic is called Golgotha). ¹⁸Here they crucified him, and with him two others—one on each side and Jesus in the middle.

¹⁹Pilate had a notice prepared and fastened to the cross. It read: JESUS OF NAZA-RETH, THE KING OF THE JEWS. ²⁰Many of the Jews read this sign, for the place where Jesus was crucified was near the city, and the sign was written in Aramaic, Latin and Greek. ²¹The chief priests of the Jews protested to Pilate, "Do not write 'The King of the Jews,' but that this man claimed to be king of the Jews."

²²Pilate answered, "What I have written, I have written."

²³When the soldiers crucified Jesus, they took his clothes, dividing them into four shares, one for each of them, with the undergarment remaining. This garment was seamless, woven in one piece from top to bottom.

²⁴"Let's not tear it," they said to one another. "Let's decide by lot who will get it."

This happened that the scripture might be fulfilled which said,

> "They divided my garments among them
> and cast lots for my clothing."ᵃ

So this is what the soldiers did.

²⁵Near the cross of Jesus stood his mother, his mother's sister, Mary the wife of Clopas, and Mary Magdalene. ²⁶When Jesus saw his mother there, and the disciple whom he loved standing nearby, he said to his mother, "Dear woman, here is your son," ²⁷and to the disciple, "Here is your mother." From that time on, this disciple took her into his home.

The Death of Jesus

²⁸Later, knowing that all was now completed, and so that the Scripture would be fulfilled, Jesus said, "I am thirsty." ²⁹A jar of wine vinegar was there, so they soaked a sponge in it, put the sponge on a stalk of the hyssop plant, and lifted it to Jesus' lips. ³⁰When he had received the drink, Jesus said, "It is finished." With that, he bowed his head and gave up his spirit.

³¹Now it was the day of Preparation, and the next day was to be a special Sab-

a24 Psalm 22:18

19:17
Num 15:36
Heb 13:12

19:18
Gal 3:13
Isa 53:12

19:19
Mt 27:37
Mk 15:26
Lk 23:38

19:23,24
Ps 22:18

19:25
Mt 27:55,56
Lk 8:2,3; 24:18

19:26
Jn 2:4; 13:23
21:24

19:28
Ps 22:1-21; 69:21

19:30
Lk 23:46
Heb 10:1-14

19:31
Num 28:17
Deut 21:22,23

●**19:18** Crucifixion was a Roman form of execution. The condemned man was forced to carry his cross along a main road to the execution site, as a warning to the people. Crosses and methods of crucifixion varied. Jesus was nailed to his cross; some people were tied with ropes. Death came by suffocation because the weight of the body made breathing difficult as the victim lost strength. Crucifixion was a hideously slow and painful death.

19:19 This sign was meant to be ironic. A king, stripped naked and executed in public view, had obviously lost his kingdom forever. But Jesus, who turns the world's wisdom upside down, was just coming into his kingdom. His death and resurrection would strike the deathblow to Satan's rule and would establish his eternal authority over the earth. Few people reading the sign that bleak afternoon understood its real meaning, but the sign was absolutely true. All was not lost. Jesus was King of the Jews—and the Gentiles, and the whole universe.

19:20 The signboard was written in three languages: Hebrew for the native Jews; Latin for the Roman occupation forces; and Greek for foreigners and Jews visiting from other lands.

19:23, 24 Roman soldiers in charge of crucifixions customarily took for themselves the clothes of the condemned men. They divided Jesus' clothing, casting lots to determine who would get his robe, the most valuable piece of clothing. This fulfilled the prophecy in Psalm 22:18.

19:25–27 Even while dying on the cross, Jesus was concerned about his family. He instructed John to care for Mary, his mother. Our families are precious gifts from God, and we should value and care for them under all circumstances. Neither Christian work nor key responsibilities in any job or position excuse us from caring for our families. What can you do today to show your love to your family?

19:27 Jesus asked his close friend John, the writer of this Gospel, to care for his mother, Mary, whose husband, Joseph, was probably dead by this time. Why didn't Jesus assign this task to his brothers? As the eldest son, Jesus entrusted his mother to a person who stayed with him at the cross—and that was John.

19:29 This vinegar was a cheap wine that the Roman soldiers drank while waiting for those being crucified to die.

19:30 Until this time, a complicated system of sacrifices atoned for sins. Sin separates people from God, and only through the sacrifice of an animal, a substitute, could people be forgiven of sin and become clean before God. But people sin continually, so frequent sacrifices were required. Jesus, however, became the final and ultimate sacrifice for sin. The word *finished* is the same as "paid in full." Jesus came to *finish* God's work of salvation (4:34; 17:4), to pay the full penalty for our sins. With his death, the complex sacrificial system ended because Jesus took all sin upon himself. Now we can freely approach God because of what Jesus did for us. Those who believe in Jesus' death and resurrection can live eternally with God and escape the penalty that comes from sin.

19:31 It was against God's law to leave the body of a dead person exposed overnight (Deuteronomy 21:23), and it was also against the law to work after sundown on Friday, when the Sabbath began. This is why the religious leaders urgently wanted to get Jesus' body off the cross and buried by sundown.

19:31–35 These Romans were experienced soldiers. They knew

bath. Because the Jews did not want the bodies left on the crosses during the Sabbath, they asked Pilate to have the legs broken and the bodies taken down. 32The soldiers therefore came and broke the legs of the first man who had been crucified with Jesus, and then those of the other. 33But when they came to Jesus and found that he was already dead, they did not break his legs. 34Instead, one of the soldiers pierced Jesus' side with a spear, bringing a sudden flow of blood and water. 35The man who saw it has given testimony, and his testimony is true. He knows that he tells the truth, and he testifies so that you also may believe. 36These things happened so that the scripture would be fulfilled: "Not one of his bones will be broken,"*a* 37and, as another scripture says, "They will look on the one they have pierced."*b*

The Burial of Jesus

38Later, Joseph of Arimathea asked Pilate for the body of Jesus. Now Joseph was a disciple of Jesus, but secretly because he feared the Jews. With Pilate's permission, he came and took the body away. 39He was accompanied by Nicodemus, the man who earlier had visited Jesus at night. Nicodemus brought a mixture of myrrh and aloes, about seventy-five pounds.*c* 40Taking Jesus' body, the two of them wrapped it, with the spices, in strips of linen. This was in accordance with Jewish burial customs. 41At the place where Jesus was crucified, there was a garden, and in the garden a new tomb, in which no one had ever been laid. 42Because it was the Jewish day of Preparation and since the tomb was nearby, they laid Jesus there.

The Empty Tomb

20 Early on the first day of the week, while it was still dark, Mary Magdalene went to the tomb and saw that the stone had been removed from the entrance. 2So she came running to Simon Peter and the other disciple, the one Jesus loved,

a36 Exodus 12:46; Num. 9:12; Psalm 34:20   *b37* Zech. 12:10   *c39* Greek *a hundred litrai* (about 34 kilograms)

19:35
Jn 20:30,31
21:24
1 Jn 1:1

19:36,37
Ex 12:46
Num 9:12
Ps 34:20
Zech 12:10
Rev 1:7

19:39
2 Chron 16:13, 14
Mt 26:12
Mk 14:8
Jn 3:1,2; 7:50
12:7

19:40
Lk 23:56
Jn 11:44

19:41
Mt 27:60
Lk 23:52

20:2
Jn 13:23

---

from many previous crucifixions whether a man was dead or alive. There was no question that Jesus was dead when they checked him, so they decided not to break his legs as they had done to the other victims. Piercing his side and seeing the separation of blood and water was further proof of his death. Some people say Jesus didn't really die, that he only passed out—and that's how he "came back to life." But we have the witness of an impartial party, the Roman soldiers, that Jesus died on the cross (Mark 15:44, 45).

19:32 The Roman soldiers broke victims' legs to hurry the death process. When a person hung on a cross, death came by suffocation, but the victim could push against the cross with his legs to hold up his body and keep breathing. With broken legs, he would suffocate immediately.

19:34, 35 The graphic details of Jesus' death are especially important in John's record because he was an eyewitness.

19:36, 37 Jesus died when the lambs for the Passover meal were being slain. Not a bone was to be broken in these sacrificial lambs (Exodus 12:46; Numbers 9:12). Jesus, the Lamb of God, was the perfect sacrifice for the sins of the world (1 Corinthians 5:7).

●**19:38–42** Joseph of Arimathea and Nicodemus were secret followers of Jesus. They were afraid to make this known because of their positions in the Jewish community. Joseph was a leader and honored member of the Jewish council. Nicodemus, also a member of the council, had come to Jesus by night (3:1) and later tried to defend him before the other religious leaders (7:50–52). Yet they risked their reputations to bury Jesus. Are you a secret believer? Do you hide your faith from your friends and fellow workers? This is an appropriate time to step out of hiding and let others know whom you follow.

19:38, 39 Four people were changed in the process of Jesus' death. The criminal, dying on the cross beside Jesus, asked Jesus to include him in his kingdom (Luke 23:39–43). The Roman captain

proclaimed that surely Jesus was the Son of God (Mark 15:39). Joseph and Nicodemus, members of the Jewish council and secret followers of Jesus (7:50–52), came out of hiding. These men were changed more by Christ's death than by his life. They realized who he was, and that realization brought out their belief, proclamation, and action. When confronted with Jesus and his death, we should be changed—to believe, proclaim, and act.

19:42 This tomb was probably a cave carved out of the stone hillside. It was large enough for a man to walk into, so Joseph and Nicodemus carried Jesus' body into it. A large stone was rolled in front of the entrance.

19:42 As they buried Jesus, Nicodemus and Joseph had to hurry to avoid working on the Sabbath, which began Friday evening at sundown.

20:1 Other women came to the tomb along with Mary Magdalene. The other Gospel accounts give their names. For more information on Mary Magdalene, see her Profile in John 20.

20:1 The stone was not rolled away from the entrance to the tomb so Jesus could get out. He could have left easily without moving the stone. It was rolled away so others could get *in* and see that Jesus was gone.

●**20:1ff** People who hear about the resurrection for the first time may need time before they can comprehend this amazing story. Like Mary and the disciples, they may pass through four stages of belief. (1) At first, they may think it is a fabrication, impossible to believe (20:2). (2) Like Peter, they may check out the facts and still be puzzled about what happened (20:6). (3) Only when they encounter Jesus personally are they able to accept the fact of the resurrection (20:16). (4) Then, as they commit themselves to the risen Lord and devote their lives to serving him, they begin to understand fully the reality of his presence with them (20:28).

and said, "They have taken the Lord out of the tomb, and we don't know where they have put him!"

3So Peter and the other disciple started for the tomb. 4Both were running, but the other disciple outran Peter and reached the tomb first. 5He bent over and looked in at the strips of linen lying there but did not go in. 6Then Simon Peter, who was behind him, arrived and went into the tomb. He saw the strips of linen lying there, 7as well as the burial cloth that had been around Jesus' head. The cloth was folded up by itself, separate from the linen. 8Finally the other disciple, who had reached the tomb first, also went inside. He saw and believed. 9(They still did not understand from Scripture that Jesus had to rise from the dead.)

20:3
Lk 24:12
20:5
Jn 19:40
20:6
Lk 24:12
20:7
Jn 11:44; 19:40
20:9
Ps 2:7; 16:8-11

Jesus Appears to Mary Magdalene

10Then the disciples went back to their homes, 11but Mary stood outside the tomb crying. As she wept, she bent over to look into the tomb 12and saw two angels in white, seated where Jesus' body had been, one at the head and the other at the foot.

20:12
Mt 28:2
Mk 16:5
Lk 24:4

13They asked her, "Woman, why are you crying?"

"They have taken my Lord away," she said, "and I don't know where they have put him." 14At this, she turned around and saw Jesus standing there, but she did not realize that it was Jesus.

20:14
Mt 28:9
Mk 16:9
Jn 21:4

15"Woman," he said, "why are you crying? Who is it you are looking for?"

Thinking he was the gardener, she said, "Sir, if you have carried him away, tell me where you have put him, and I will get him."

16Jesus said to her, "Mary."

She turned toward him and cried out in Aramaic, "Rabboni!" (which means Teacher).

17Jesus said, "Do not hold on to me, for I have not yet returned to the Father. Go instead to my brothers and tell them, 'I am returning to my Father and your Father, to my God and your God.' "

20:17
Mt 28:10
Jn 16:28
Rom 8:29
Col 1:18
Heb 2:11
1 Pet 1:3

18Mary Magdalene went to the disciples with the news: "I have seen the Lord!" And she told them that he had said these things to her.

Jesus Appears to His Disciples

19On the evening of that first day of the week, when the disciples were together, with the doors locked for fear of the Jews, Jesus came and stood among them and said, "Peace be with you!" 20After he said this, he showed them his hands and side. The disciples were overjoyed when they saw the Lord.

20:19
Lk 24:36-43

21Again Jesus said, "Peace be with you! As the Father has sent me, I am sending

20:21
Mt 28:18-20

20:7 The grave clothes were left as if Jesus had passed right through them. The head piece was still rolled up in the shape of a head, and it was at about the right distance from the wrappings that had enveloped Jesus' body. A grave robber couldn't possibly have made off with Jesus' body and left the linens as if they were still shaped around it.

20:9 As further proof that the disciples did not fabricate this story, we find that Peter and John were surprised that Jesus was not in the tomb. When John saw the grave clothes looking like an empty cocoon from which Jesus had emerged, he believed Jesus had risen. It wasn't until after they had seen the empty tomb that they remembered what the Scriptures and Jesus had said—he would die, but he would also rise again!

20:9 Jesus' resurrection is the key to the Christian faith. Why? (1) Just as he said, Jesus rose from the dead. We can be confident, therefore, that he will accomplish all he has promised. (2) Jesus' bodily resurrection shows us that the living Christ, not a false prophet or imposter, is ruler of God's eternal kingdom. (3) We can be certain of our own resurrection because Jesus was resurrected. Death is not the end—there is future life. (4) The divine power that brought Jesus back to life is now available to us to bring our spiritually dead selves back to life. (5) The resurrection is the basis

for the church's witness to the world.

20:17 Mary did not want to lose Jesus again. She had not yet understood the resurrection. Perhaps she thought this was his promised second coming (14:3). But Jesus did not want to be detained by the tomb. If he did not ascend to heaven, the Holy Spirit could not come. Both he and Mary had important work to do.

●**20:18** Mary didn't recognize Jesus at first. Her grief had blinded her; she couldn't see him because she didn't expect to see him. Then he spoke her name, and immediately she recognized him. Imagine the love that flooded her heart when she heard her Savior saying her name. Jesus is near you, and he is calling your name. Can you, like Mary, regard him as your Lord?

20:18 Mary did not rest until she had discovered the empty tomb. She responded with joy and obedience in telling the disciples. We cannot meet Christ until we discover that he is indeed alive, that his tomb is empty. Are we filled with joy by this good news, and do we share it with others?

●**20:21** Jesus again identified himself with his Father. He told the disciples by whose authority he did his work. Now he passed the job to his disciples of spreading the gospel of salvation around the world. Whatever God has asked you to do, remember: (1) your authority comes from God, and (2) Jesus has demonstrated by words

20:22
Jn 7:37-39
14:16-18,26

you." 22And with that he breathed on them and said, "Receive the Holy Spirit. 23If you forgive anyone his sins, they are forgiven; if you do not forgive them, they are not forgiven."

Jesus Appears to Thomas

24Now Thomas (called Didymus), one of the Twelve, was not with the disciples

---

MARY MAGDALENE

The absence of women among the 12 disciples has bothered a few people. But it is clear that there were many women among Jesus' followers. It is also clear that Jesus did not treat women as others in his culture did; he treated them with dignity, as people with worth.

Mary Magdalene was an early follower of Jesus and certainly deserves to be called a disciple. An energetic, impulsive, caring woman, she not only traveled with Jesus, but also contributed to the needs of the group. She was present at the crucifixion and was on her way to embalm Jesus' body on Sunday morning when she discovered the empty tomb. Mary was the first to see Jesus after his resurrection.

Mary Magdalene is a heartwarming example of thankful living. Her life was miraculously freed by Jesus when he cast seven demons out of her. In every glimpse we have of her, she was acting out her appreciation for the freedom Christ had given her. That freedom allowed her to stand under Christ's cross when all the disciples except John were hiding in fear. After Jesus' death, she intended to give his body every respect. Like the rest of Jesus' followers, she never expected his bodily resurrection—but she was overjoyed to discover it.

Mary's faith was not complicated, but it was direct and genuine. She was more eager to believe and obey than to understand everything. Jesus honored her childlike faith by appearing to her first and by entrusting her with the first message of his resurrection.

Strengths and accomplishments:
● Contributed to the needs of Jesus and his disciples
● One of the few faithful followers present at Jesus' death on the cross
● First to see the risen Christ

Weakness and mistake:
● Jesus had to cast seven demons out of her

Lessons from her life:
● Those who are obedient grow in understanding
● Women are vital to Jesus' ministry
● Jesus relates to women as he created them—as equal reflectors of God's image

Vital statistics:
● Where: Magdala
● Occupation: We are not told, but she seems to have been wealthy
● Contemporaries: Jesus, the 12 disciples, Mary, Martha, Lazarus, Jesus' mother Mary

Key verse:
"When Jesus rose early on the first day of the week, he appeared first to Mary Magdalene, out of whom he had driven seven demons" (Mark 16:9).

Mary Magdalene's story is told in Matthew 27; 28; Mark 15; 16; Luke 23; 24; and John 19; 20. She is also mentioned in Luke 8:2.

---

and actions how to accomplish the job he has given you. As the Father sent Jesus, Jesus sends his followers.

20:22 This is a special filling of the Holy Spirit for the disciples, a foretaste of what all believers would experience from the time of Pentecost (Acts 2) and forever after. To do God's work, we need the guidance and power of the Holy Spirit. We must avoid trying to do his work in our own strength.

20:22 There is life in the breath of God. Man was created but did not come alive until God breathed into him the breath of life (Genesis 2:7). His first breath made man different from all other forms of creation. Now, through the breath of Jesus, God imparted eternal, spiritual life and the power to do God's will on earth.

20:23 Jesus is telling the disciples their Spirit-powered and Spirit-guided mission—to preach the Good News about Jesus so peo-

ple's sins might be forgiven. The disciples did not have the power to forgive sins (only God can forgive sins), but Jesus gave them the privilege of telling new believers that their sins *have been* forgiven because they have accepted Jesus' message. All believers have this same privilege. We can announce the forgiveness of sin with certainty when we ourselves find repentance and faith.

●**20:24–29** Have you ever wished you could actually see Jesus, touch him, hear his words, and get his advice? Thomas wanted Jesus' physical presence. But God's plan is wiser. He has not limited himself to one physical body; he wants to be present with you at all times. Even now he is with you in the form of the Holy Spirit. You can talk to him, and you can find his words to you in the pages of the Bible. He can be as real to you as he was to Thomas.

when Jesus came. 25So the other disciples told him, "We have seen the Lord!"

But he said to them, "Unless I see the nail marks in his hands and put my finger where the nails were, and put my hand into his side, I will not believe it."

26A week later his disciples were in the house again, and Thomas was with them. Though the doors were locked, Jesus came and stood among them and said, "Peace be with you!" 27Then he said to Thomas, "Put your finger here; see my hands. Reach out your hand and put it into my side. Stop doubting and believe."

28Thomas said to him, "My Lord and my God!"

29Then Jesus told him, "Because you have seen me, you have believed; blessed are those who have not seen and yet have believed."

30Jesus did many other miraculous signs in the presence of his disciples, which are not recorded in this book. 31But these are written that you may*a* believe that Jesus is the Christ, the Son of God, and that by believing you may have life in his name.

Jesus and the Miraculous Catch of Fish

21 Afterward Jesus appeared again to his disciples, by the Sea of Tiberias. *b* It happened this way: 2Simon Peter, Thomas (called Didymus), Nathanael from Cana in Galilee, the sons of Zebedee, and two other disciples were together. 3"I'm going out to fish," Simon Peter told them, and they said, "We'll go with you." So they went out and got into the boat, but that night they caught nothing.

4Early in the morning, Jesus stood on the shore, but the disciples did not realize that it was Jesus.

5He called out to them, "Friends, haven't you any fish?"

"No," they answered.

6He said, "Throw your net on the right side of the boat and you will find some." When they did, they were unable to haul the net in because of the large number of fish.

7Then the disciple whom Jesus loved said to Peter, "It is the Lord!" As soon as Simon Peter heard him say, "It is the Lord," he wrapped his outer garment around him (for he had taken it off) and jumped into the water. 8The other disciples followed in the boat, towing the net full of fish, for they were not far from shore, about a hundred yards. *c* 9When they landed, they saw a fire of burning coals there with fish on it, and some bread.

10Jesus said to them, "Bring some of the fish you have just caught."

11Simon Peter climbed aboard and dragged the net ashore. It was full of large fish, 153, but even with so many the net was not torn. 12Jesus said to them, "Come and have breakfast." None of the disciples dared ask him, "Who are you?" They knew it was the Lord. 13Jesus came, took the bread and gave it to them, and did the

a31 Some manuscripts may continue to   b1 That is, Sea of Galilee   c8 Greek about two hundred cubits (about 90 meters)

Marginal references:
20:24 Jn 11:16
20:28 Jn 1:1,18 10:30; 14:9 Phil 2:6 Col 2:9 Tit 2:13 2 Pet 1:1 1 Jn 5:20
20:29 2 Cor 5:7 1 Pet 1:8
20:30,31 Jn 3:15,16 5:24; 19:35 21:25
21:1 Jn 21:14
21:2 Mt 4:21,22 Jn 1:45-51
21:6 Lk 5:4-7
21:7 Jn 13:21; 21:20
21:9 Jn 6:9,11
21:12 Acts 10:41

●**20:25–28** Jesus wasn't hard on Thomas for his doubts. Despite his skepticism, Thomas was still loyal to the believers and to Jesus himself. Some need to doubt before they believe. If doubt leads to questions, the questions lead to answers, and the answers are accepted, then doubt has done good work. It is when doubt becomes stubbornness and stubbornness becomes a life-style that doubt harms faith. When you doubt, don't stop there. Let your doubt deepen your faith as you continue to search for the answer.

20:27 Jesus' resurrected body was not the same kind of flesh and blood Lazarus had when he came back to life. Jesus' body was no longer subject to the same laws of nature as before his death. He could appear in a locked room, yet he was not a ghost or apparition; he could be touched and could eat. Jesus' resurrection was *literal* and *physical*—he was not a disembodied spirit.

20:29 Some people think they would believe in Jesus if they could see a definite sign or miracle. But Jesus says we are blessed if we

can believe without seeing. We have all the proof we need in the Bible and the testimony of believers. A physical appearance would not make Jesus any more real to us than he is now.

20:30, 31 To understand the life and mission of Jesus more fully, all we need to do is study the Gospels. John tells us that his Gospel records only a few of the many events in Jesus' life on earth. But the Gospel includes everything we need to know to believe that Jesus is the Christ, the Son of God, through whom we receive eternal life.

21:1ff This chapter tells how Jesus commissioned Peter. Perhaps Peter needed special encouragement after his denial—he may have felt completely worthless. Verses 1–14 set the scene for Jesus' conversation with Peter.

21:7 Only John recognized Jesus in the dim morning light, undoubtedly because Jesus had performed a similar miracle earlier (Luke 5:1–11).

21:14
Jn 20:19,26

same with the fish. 14This was now the third time Jesus appeared to his disciples after he was raised from the dead.

Jesus Reinstates Peter

21:15
Mt 26:33

15When they had finished eating, Jesus said to Simon Peter, "Simon son of John, do you truly love me more than these?"

Thomas, so often remembered as "Doubting Thomas," deserves to be respected for his faith. He was a doubter, but his doubts had a purpose—he wanted to know the truth. Thomas did not idolize his doubts; he gladly believed when given reasons to do so. He expressed his doubts fully and had them answered completely. Doubting was only his way of responding, not his way of life.

Although our glimpses of Thomas are brief, his character comes through with consistency. He struggled to be faithful to what he knew, despite what he felt. At one point, when it was plain to everyone that Jesus' life was in danger, only Thomas put into words what most were feeling, "Let us also go, that we may die with him" (John 11:16). He didn't hesitate to follow Jesus.

We don't know why Thomas was absent the first time Jesus appeared to the disciples after the resurrection, but he was reluctant to believe their witness to Christ's resurrection. Not even 10 friends could change his mind!

We can doubt without having to live a doubting way of life. Doubt encourages rethinking. Its purpose is more to sharpen the mind than to change it. Doubt can be used to pose the question, get an answer, and push for a decision. But doubt was never meant to be a permanent condition. Doubt is one foot lifted, poised to step forward or back. There is no motion until the foot comes down.

When you experience doubt, take encouragement from Thomas. He didn't stay in his doubt, but allowed Jesus to bring him to belief. Take encouragement also from the fact that countless other followers of Christ have struggled with doubts. The answers God gave them may help you too. Don't settle into doubts, but move on from them to decision and belief. Find another believer with whom you can share your doubts. Silent doubts rarely find answers.

Strengths and accomplishments:
- One of Jesus' 12 disciples
- Intense both in doubt and belief
- Was a loyal and honest man

Weaknesses and mistakes:
- Along with the others, abandoned Jesus at his arrest
- Refused to believe the others' claims to have seen Christ and demanded proof
- Struggled with a pessimistic outlook

Lessons from his life:
- Jesus does not reject doubts that are honest and directed toward belief
- Better to doubt out loud than to disbelieve in silence

Vital statistics:
- Where: Galilee, Judea, Samaria
- Occupation: Disciple of Jesus
- Contemporaries: Jesus, other disciples, Herod, Pilate

Key verses:
"Then he said to Thomas, 'Put your finger here; see my hands. Reach out your hand and put it into my side. Stop doubting and believe.' Thomas said to him, 'My Lord and my God!'" (John 20:27, 28).

Thomas's story is told in the Gospels. He is also mentioned in Acts 1:13.

21:15–17 In this beach scene, Jesus led Peter through an experience that would remove the cloud of his denial. Peter had denied Jesus three times. Three times Jesus asked Peter if he loved him. When Peter answered yes, Jesus told him to feed his sheep. It is one thing to say you love Jesus, but the real test is willingness to serve him. Peter had repented, and now Jesus asked him to commit his life. Peter's life changed when he finally realized who Jesus was. His occupation changed from fisherman to evangelist; his identity changed from impetuous to "rock," and his relationship to Jesus changed—now he was forgiven and fully understood the significance of Jesus' words about his death and resurrection.

●**21:15–17** Jesus asked Peter three times if he loved him. The first time Jesus said, "Do you truly love (Greek *agape:* volitional, self-sacrificial love) me more than these?" The second time, Jesus focused on Peter alone and still used the word translated into Greek, *agape.* The third time, Jesus used the word translated into Greek, *phileo* (signifying affection, affinity, or brotherly love) and asked, in effect, "Are you even my friend?" Each time Peter responded with the word translated into Greek as *phileo.* Jesus doesn't settle for quick, superficial answers. He has a way of getting to the heart of the matter. Peter had to face his true feelings and motives when Jesus confronted him. How would you respond if Jesus asked you, "Do you truly love me?" Do you really love Jesus? Are you his friend?

"Yes, Lord," he said, "you know that I love you."

Jesus said, "Feed my lambs."

16Again Jesus said, "Simon son of John, do you truly love me?"
He answered, "Yes, Lord, you know that I love you."

Jesus said, "Take care of my sheep."

17The third time he said to him, "Simon son of John, do you love me?"
Peter was hurt because Jesus asked him the third time, "Do you love me?" He
said, "Lord, you know all things; you know that I love you."

Jesus said, "Feed my sheep. 18I tell you the truth, when you were younger you
dressed yourself and went where you wanted; but when you are old you will stretch
out your hands, and someone else will dress you and lead you where you do not
want to go." 19Jesus said this to indicate the kind of death by which Peter would
glorify God. Then he said to him, "Follow me!"

20Peter turned and saw that the disciple whom Jesus loved was following them.
(This was the one who had leaned back against Jesus at the supper and had said,
"Lord, who is going to betray you?") 21When Peter saw him, he asked, "Lord, what
about him?"

22Jesus answered, "If I want him to remain alive until I return, what is that to
you? You must follow me." 23Because of this, the rumor spread among the brothers
that this disciple would not die. But Jesus did not say that he would not die; he only
said, "If I want him to remain alive until I return, what is that to you?"

24This is the disciple who testifies to these things and who wrote them down. We
know that his testimony is true.

25Jesus did many other things as well. If every one of them were written down,
I suppose that even the whole world would not have room for the books that would
be written.

21:16
Heb 13:20,21
1 Pet 2:25,5:2

21:17
1 Chron 28:9
29:17
2 Chron 6:30
Jer 17:10
Jn 2:24,25
13:38
Rom 8:27
1 Thess 2:4

21:19
2 Pet 1:13,14

21:20
Jn 13:23-25

21:22
Deut 29:29
1 Cor 4:5; 11:26
Rev 2:25; 3:11
22:7,20

21:24
Jn 1:14; 15:27
19:35
1 Jn 1:1-3
3 Jn 12

21:25
Jn 20:30,31

		JESUS'
Mary Magdalene	Mark 16:9–11; John 20:10–18	**APPEARANCES**
The other women at the tomb	Matthew 28:8–10	**AFTER HIS**
Peter in Jerusalem	Luke 24:34; 1 Corinthians 15:5	**RESURRECTION**
The two travelers on the road	Mark 16:12, 13	
Ten disciples behind closed doors	Mark 16:14; Luke 24:36–43; John 20:19–25	
All the disciples, with Thomas (excluding Judas Iscariot)	John 20:26–31; 1 Corinthians 15:5	
Seven disciples while fishing	John 21:1–14	
Eleven disciples on the mountain	Matthew 28:16–20	
A crowd of 500	1 Corinthians 15:6	
His brother James	1 Corinthians 15:7	
Those who watched him ascend into heaven	Luke 24:44–49; Acts 1:3–8	

The truth of Christianity rests heavily on the resurrection. If Jesus rose from the grave, who saw him? How
trustworthy were the witnesses? Those who claimed to have seen the risen Jesus went on to turn the world
upside down. Most of them also died for being followers of Christ. People rarely die for half-hearted belief.
These are the people who saw Jesus risen from the grave.

21:18, 19 This was a prediction of Peter's death by crucifixion.
Tradition indicates that Peter was crucified for his faith—upside
down because he did not feel worthy of dying as his Lord did. Despite what his future held, Jesus told Peter to follow him. We may
be uncertain and fearful about our future. But if we know God is in
control, we can confidently follow Christ.

21:21, 22 Peter asked Jesus what would happen to John. Jesus
replied that Peter should not concern himself with that. We tend to
compare our lives to those of others, whether to rationalize our own
level of devotion to Christ or to question God's justice. Jesus re-
sponds to us as he did to Peter: "What is that to you? You must follow me."

21:23 Early church history reports that John, after spending several years as an exile on the island of Patmos, returned to Ephe-
sus, where he died as an old man near the end of the first century.

●**21:25** John's stated purpose for writing his Gospel was to show
that Jesus was the Son of God. He clearly and systematically presented the evidence for Jesus' claims. When evidence is presented in the courtroom, those who hear it must make a choice.
Those who read the Gospel of John must also make a choice—is
Jesus the Son of God, or isn't he? You are the jury. The evidence
has been clearly presented. You must decide. Read John's Gospel
and believe!

JESUS' MIRACLES

John and the other Gospel writers were able to record only a fraction of the people who were touched and healed by Jesus. But enough of Jesus' words and works have been saved so that we also might be able to know him and be his disciples in this day. There follows a listing of the miracles that are included in the Gospels. They were supernatural events that pointed people to God, and they were acts of love by one who is love.

	Matthew	Mark	Luke	John
Five thousand people are fed	14:15–21	6:35–44	9:12–17	6:5–14
Calming the storm	8:23–27	4:35–41	8:22–25	
Demons sent into the pigs	8:28–34	5:1–20	8:26–39	
Jairus's daughter raised	9:18–26	5:22–24, 35–43	8:41, 42, 49–56	
A sick woman is healed	9:20–22	5:25–34	8:43–48	
Jesus heals a paralytic	9:1–8	2:1–12	5:17–26	
A leper is healed at Gennesaret	8:1–4	1:40–45	5:12–15	
Peter's mother-in-law healed	8:14–17	1:29–31	4:38, 39	
A shriveled hand is restored	12:9–13	3:1–5	6:6–11	
A boy with an evil spirit is cured	17:14–21	9:14–29	9:37–42	
Jesus walks on the water	14:22–33	6:45–52		6:17–21
Blind Bartimaeus receives sight	20:29–34	10:46–52	18:35–43	
A girl is freed from a demon	15:21–28	7:24–30		
Four thousand are fed	15:32–38	8:1–9		
Cursing the fig tree	21:18–22	11:12–14, 20–24		
A centurion's servant is healed	8:5–13		7:1–10	
An evil spirit is sent out of a man		1:23–27	4:33–36	
A mute demoniac is healed	12:22		11:14	
Two blind men find sight	9:27–31			
Jesus heals the mute man	9:32, 33			
A coin in a fish's mouth	17:24–27			
A deaf and mute man is healed		7:31–37		
A blind man sees at Bethsaida		8:22–26		
The first miraculous catch of fish			5:1–11	
A widow's son is raised			7:11–16	
A crippled woman is healed			13:10–17	
Jesus heals a sick man			14:1–6	
Ten lepers are healed			17:11–19	
Jesus restores a man's ear			22:49–51	
Jesus turns water into wine				2:1–11
An official's son is healed at Cana				4:46–54
A lame man is healed				5:1–16
Jesus heals a man born blind				9:1–7
Lazarus is raised from the dead				11:1–45
The second miraculous catch of fish				21:1–14

COMPARISON OF THE FOUR GOSPELS

All four Gospels present the life and teachings of Jesus. Each book, however, focuses on a unique facet of Jesus and his character. To understand more about the specific characteristics of Jesus, read any one of the four Gospels.

	Matthew	Mark	Luke	John
Jesus is . . .	The promised King	The Servant of God	The Son of Man	The Son of God
The original readers were . . .	Jews	Gentiles, Romans	Greeks	Christians throughout the world
Significant themes . . .	Jesus is the Messiah because he fulfilled Old Testament prophecy	Jesus backed up his words with action	Jesus was God but also fully human	Belief in Jesus is required for salvation
Character of the writer . . .	Teacher	Storyteller	Historian	Theologian
Greatest emphasis is on . . .	Jesus' sermons and words	Jesus' miracles and actions	Jesus' humanity	The principles of Jesus' teaching

Prayer Requests

Darcel - finances, direction
  year - balance of time for prayer, study

Mary Kay - forgiveness to those who have sinned against her.

Kathryn - for Connor, strength for Kathryn, peace about his life - discipline and time for study & prayer. : healing

Colleen - prayer for marriage - doesn't want to be married anymore. (Joe)

Krissy - for husband, Tom, to be a believer
  - struggles w/ judging & being too hard on him.
  - needs faith that God is working on Tom's heart, ~~know together~~ also to be silent toward him.

Mickey - for health

It's always exciting to get more than you expect. And that's what you'll find in this Bible study guide—much more than you expect. Our goal was to write thoughtful, practical, dependable, and application-oriented studies of God's Word.

This study guide contains the complete text of the selected Bible book. The commentary is accurate, complete, and loaded with unique charts, maps, and profiles of Bible people.

With the Bible text, extensive notes and helps, and questions to guide discussion, these Life Application Study Guides have everything you need in one place.

The lessons in this Bible study guide will work for large classes as well as small-group studies. To get everyone involved in your discussions, encourage participants to answer the questions before each meeting.

Each lesson is divided into five easy-to-lead sections. The section called "Reflect" introduces you and the members of your group to a specific area of life touched by the lesson. "Read" shows which chapters to read and which notes and other features to use. Additional questions help you understand the passage. "Realize" brings into focus the biblical principle to be learned with questions, a special insight, or both. "Respond" helps you make connections with your own situation and personal needs. The questions are designed to help you find areas in your life where you can apply the biblical truths. "Resolve" helps you map out action plans for that day.

Begin and end each lesson with prayer, asking for the Holy Spirit's guidance, direction, and wisdom.

Recommended time allotments for each section of a lesson:

Segment	60 minutes	90 minutes
Reflect on your life	5 minutes	10 minutes
Read the passage	10 minutes	15 minutes
Realize the principle	15 minutes	20 minutes
Respond to the message	20 minutes	30 minutes
Resolve to take action	10 minutes	15 minutes

All five sections work together to help a person learn the lessons, live out the principles, and obey the commands taught in the Bible.

Also, at the end of each lesson, there is a section entitled, "More for studying other themes in this section." These questions will help you lead the group in studying other parts of each section not covered in depth by the main lesson.

Do not merely listen to the word, and so deceive yourselves. Do what it says. Anyone who listens to the word but does not do what it says is like a man who looks at his face in a mirror and, after looking at himself, goes away and immediately forgets what he looks like. But the man who looks intently into the perfect law that gives freedom, and continues to do this, not forgetting what he has heard, but doing it—he will be blessed in what he does. (James 1:22-25, NIV)

STUDY QUESTIONS

Thirteen lessons for individual or group study

REFLECT
on your life

1 What makes you have high confidence in someone?

_____

_____

_____

2 What makes you lose confidence in someone?

_____

_____

_____

READ
the passage

Read the three pages of introductory material to John. Note the Key Verse under Vital Statistics. Become familiar with the land of Israel by tracing the travels of Jesus on the map.

3 What was John's purpose for writing this Gospel?

_____

_____

_____

_____

4 What kind of evidence do people need to convince them that Jesus is God's Son?

_____

_____

_____

_____

_____

_____

5 What different types of evidence does John give?

_____

_____

_____

_____

6 What evidence for the deity of Christ could you present to someone if asked?

_____

_____

_____

_____

REALIZE
the principle

The Gospel of John is a study of God's love for us in sending his Son, Jesus Christ. For three years John was one of the disciples closest to Jesus. He saw everything Jesus did and heard everything he said. John said he wrote his Gospel to present eyewitness evidence of the deity of Christ so that we may believe and have eternal life. If you are unsure of your faith or the claims of Christ, this book will give you the evidence you need to decide for Christ. If you are already a believer, this study will boost your confidence.

7 List some of your questions about God, Jesus, the Bible, or the Christian faith that you always wanted to ask but didn't know whom to ask.

_____

_____

RESPOND
to the message

8 How might this study of John help answer those questions?

9 Which question is most important to you?

10 What might you do this week to begin exploring this question?

RESOLVE
to take action

11 What people or information resources can you tap this week that might provide an answer to your question?

A What do you hope to gain from this study of John? How would you like your life to be different after studying and applying the truths in this book?

MORE
for studying
other themes
in this section

B If someone accused you in a court of law of being a Christian, what evidence could they use to prove their claim?

C If your home were dug up 1000 years from now, what would the evidence say about you?

D What is eternal life? How can someone receive eternal life? What difference does it make *now* to have life after death?

E How does a person receive the Holy Spirit? What does the Holy Spirit do in the world? In our lives? How can you live in the power of the Spirit?

REFLECT
on your life

1 Describe yourself without referring to your appearance, career, or accomplishments.

simple, kind, easy-going,
undisciplined,

2 How would you describe God to a person who has never been to church?

all knowing, loving, creator,
forgiving, approachable, His
ways are perfect, gives peace

READ
the passage

Read John 1:1-34 and the following notes:

☐1:1 ☐1:3-5 ☐1:4 ☐1:4,5 ☐1:8 ☐1:14 ☐1:18 ☐1:29

3 What are some of the words John (the Gospel writer) uses to describe Christ?

the Word, light, One & Only, full of grace &
truth, the Lord, Lamb of God,

4 In what ways do people live in darkness?

by ~~night~~ not accepting Jesus as lord
and Savior, or not allowing the light
— Jesus — in their life.
— not knowing Jesus personally.

REALIZE
the principle

Communication is difficult without having common experiences or understanding. Ideas may be interesting, but they must be fleshed out to be meaningful. God became flesh in Jesus Christ. No longer do we have to guess what God is like or just discuss him as a concept. Jesus is God come to earth to take away our sins and to give us new life. If God cares that much about us, we can trust him with our daily concerns. Because Jesus is God, we know that what he says is true; we know that his death on the cross really was for sin; and we know that we should obey him and imitate his life.

5 How are Jesus' words and life unique?

He's God, so we have a direct line to Him,
and understanding of who God is. We can
know God fully — He is the perfect teacher,
perfect example, perfect sacrifice

6 How are his words and life common to all human beings?

He walked on earth & talked with people
He taught

7 How does Jesus' life help you know what God is like?

Because Jesus is God I can see the love
He demonstrated for me while on earth
— that short time — and know that His
love is eternal for me. God became "tangible"
for me.

RESPOND
to the message

8 What difference does it make to your faith that God walked on earth in a human body?

He became like me-so I know He understads me because " He's been there." He knows my needs, so Hesupplies them.

v. 32 **9** What evidence for the deity of Jesus does John appeal to in these verses?

" The Spirit came down from heaver as a dove and remained on Him."

10 What difference does it make to your faith that Jesus is God?

that makes my faith. He died for me sins! where would I be without His sacrifice for me?

11 As you encounter the frustrations and difficulties of daily life, remind yourself that Jesus became fully human—he experienced frustrations and feelings similar to yours. What can you carry with you this week to help you remember?

RESOLVE
to take action

MORE
for studying
other themes
in this section

A What does it mean to live in the light of Christ?

B What characteristics of God can others recognize in our lives?

C In what areas of life are you stumbling around in darkness?

D What was John the Baptist's mission in life? What qualities in the life of John the Baptist do you admire? What can you do to develop these qualities in yourself?

E According to verse 29, Jesus came to take away the world's sin. In John 1:1-34, how does this happen?

F What is new in the life of a person who has been reborn?

John 14:6-11

belief- to trust, rely on, commit to

– Ask Jesus to put in us what our children need
I need to be a child of God 1st, mom 2nd

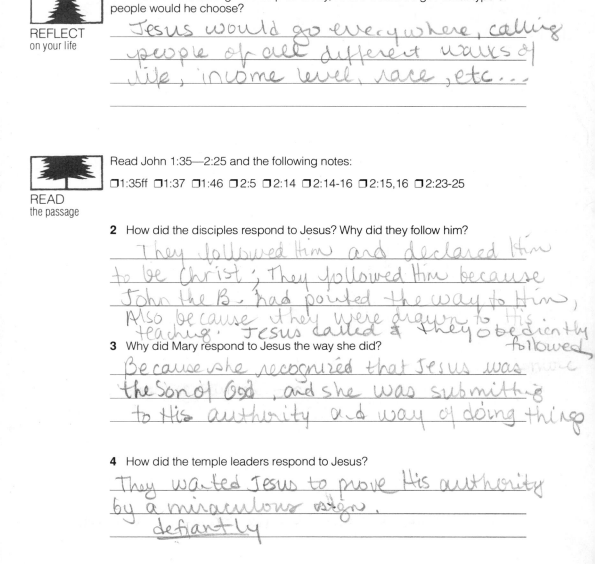

REFLECT
on your life

1 If Jesus were calling 12 disciples today, where would he go? What type of people would he choose?

Jesus would go everywhere, calling people of all different walks of life, income level, race, etc...

READ
the passage

Read John 1:35—2:25 and the following notes:

☐1:35ff ☐1:37 ☐1:46 ☐2:5 ☐2:14 ☐2:14-16 ☐2:15,16 ☐2:23-25

2 How did the disciples respond to Jesus? Why did they follow him?

They followed Him and declared Him to be Christ; They followed Him because John the B. had pointed the way to Him, Also because they were drawn to His teaching. Jesus called & they obediently followed

3 Why did Mary respond to Jesus the way she did?

Because she recognized that Jesus was the Son of God, and she was submitting to His authority and way of doing things

4 How did the temple leaders respond to Jesus?

They wanted Jesus to prove His authority by a miraculous sign.
defiantly

5 How does Jesus call disciples today? Why did you decide to follow him?

by His Word & Spirit through
Christians today. I followed Him
because I realized the "hole" in
my heart and the need I had for Him
in my life. I realized there was no way
I could ever live up to His standards
w/o Him. I needed His forgiveness and a
relief from all the guilt I had.

REALIZE
the principle

6 How did John the Baptist respond to Jesus?

obediently - after God had revealed
Jesus to Him by his spirit.

7 Give at least one modern example of each kind of response to Jesus.

Response	Biblical example	Modern example
Submission	Mary	
Obedience	disciples	
Defiance	temple leaders	
Superficiality	people at Passover	"religious" people

name or group of people

How we respond to Jesus is critical, because it can make the difference between life and death—eternally. It can affect our sense of joy and fulfillment as believers. When Andrew, John, Philip, and Nathanael responded, they became disciples—close, intimate companions of Jesus during his three years of public ministry. Belief is not the only criterion of faithfulness to God, but it is the first correct response. What you believe about Christ is fundamental. The Jewish leaders blindly practiced traditional religious rituals and at the same time conducted lucrative business in the temple. Their defensive rather than repentant response to Jesus revealed the true nature of their hearts and faith.

8 What is in our lives that could show disrespect for God?

making decisions w/o consulting His
desire; prejudging others; being
self-righteous, ignoring Him

any personal gain in the name of Christ

9 What is in our lives that shows respect for God?

Our thoughts continually being on Him — checking to see if what we are doing is pleasing or not, to Him. — living according to His ways.

RESPOND
to the message

10 What makes it difficult to follow Jesus?

the commitment it requires in time of prayer and intimate fellowship with Him. It's impossible to follow Him w/o being close, and impossible to be close if not in the Word & prayer; the 2 areas in my life that I lack discipline.

11 If you sensed that God wanted you to give up your life-long career and serve him in another way, what questions or reservations would you have?

Unfortunately, I would want to know where "I would be" a year from now, or later. I would need to know specifically how He would make things work out for me and my family. — very untrusting response!

RESOLVE
to take action

12 What response do you need to make in obedience to God this week? What do you know you should do that you have been putting off?

Just be in the Word & be praying. If I'm not doing that I will be ignorant about what God wants from (for?) me. So, that's a 1st step. I need to set up a time to do this and stick with it!

A Why did John the Baptist's disciples follow Jesus? Why did John the Baptist give up these followers? *John pointed the way to Jesus. and He knew Jesus was the Messiah.*

MORE
for studying
other themes
in this section

B How did Peter come to Christ? Who introduced you to Christ? Who have you introduced to him? *His brother, Andrew, told him. Annette Romero introduced me.*

I have introduced Him to several friends & family member. All have rejected

Jesus had authority & power

C What does the wedding incident tell us about Jesus? Why did this miracle convince the disciples that Jesus was the Messiah? What would it take to convince you?

D Why did Jesus clear out the temple? Who or what would he clear out of your church? *They were not using it as a place of worship.*

E What do Jesus' actions teach us about anger? What makes you angry?

F Why didn't Jesus entrust himself to the people at the Passover Feast (2:23, 24)?

G What evidence for the deity of Jesus does John appeal to in these verses?

John 2: 12-17

REFLECT
on your life

1 When was the last time you had to convince someone of something?

_____

_____

_____

2 What was your approach?

_____

_____

_____

READ
the passage

Read John 3:1—4:42, Nicodemus's Profile, and the following notes:

❐3:1 ❐3:3 ❐3:8 ❐3:16 ❐3:19-21 ❐3:25ff ❐3:26 ❐4:4 ❐4:5-7 ❐4:15
❐4:35 ❐4:39

3 What do we learn about Nicodemus from this passage?

he was a ruler, and a member of the Pharisees
curious about Jesus, searching for
answers

4 What do we learn about John the Baptist?

He was humble — would not stop doing what God
had called Him to do — gave glory to Jesus not
to himself

Samaritan — a hated mix race

5 What do we learn about the Samaritan woman?

She was living in sin, in a public place at a time
when the other women would not be there. She was
interested in what Jesus was sharing, but
became confused by it

6 Compare Jesus' discussion with Nicodemus to his discussion with the
Samaritan woman.

REALIZE
the principle

Nicodemus — He spoke about spiritual
rebirth, and eternal life to those who
believe / lightness & darkness
Samaritan woman — He spoke of the living water
springing up to eternal life — worshipping in
spirit & truth

7 Summarize the gospel message as found in this section.

Jesus is God's Son. We need to be born
again, of the Spirit, to have eternal
life. Not only knowing God & who
Jesus was, but to believe all that He
says and by faith & a great deal of trust
putting our lives into His hands.

John the Baptist pointed his disciples to Jesus. Understanding the role God
called him to play in the kingdom, John gave his complete loyalty and support
to Jesus. John is an excellent example of humility and single devotion. Jesus
pointed his disciples to a ripe harvest. For a group of men who were at that time
thinking only about food, Jesus' call to reach a lost world had to be convicting.
Jesus modeled what he said by pointing both Nicodemus and the Samaritan
woman to faith in God. The Scriptures still point us, as Christ's disciples today,
to reach a lost world.

RESPOND
to the message

8 What individuals come to your mind when you read Jesus' words "ripe for harvest"?

my family, childrens' parents, friends in the neighborhood

9 What happens to a person who dies without Christ?

wrath and judgment - eternal life without Jesus.

10 What happens in the daily life of a person who lives apart from Christ?

their soul hungers & thirsts for spiritual food & water - they are living in darkness, afraid to be exposed by Christs' light, therefore turning away from it even more

11 What difference does knowing Christ make in your life?

I know I am important & unconditionally loved. I can know that all things that happen in my life will all work together for good. I have a peace and a hope for eternal life w/ Jesus, and I don't need to worry about or be concerned about my eternal destination. I don't have to live alone or lonely.

12 What slows you down or stops you from sharing your faith with others?

finding the right words to use, or fear of "turning them off" from either Jesus or myself

13 Whom will you pray for this week about his/her need to find Christ?

my parents

RESOLVE
to take action

14 List two or three steps you can take this week to begin pointing this person to Christ.

praying for them, responding to mom's letter, explaining my knowledge of God's love and how that affects my life
_???_

A What evidence for the deity of Jesus does John appeal to in these verses?

B How does a person become born again? How would you explain this event to your friends? _spiritual, being alive to Christ_

C How do we know that God loves us? _Jesus_ How can we show his love to others? How can we sow for Christ? How can we reap?

D Why did Christ come to earth? _to change us on the inside & to empower us to deal w/ problems from God's perspective_

E What happened as a result of Jesus talking with the Samaritan woman? _She shared with others & many came to believe in Jesus_

MORE
for studying
other themes
in this section

LESSON 5
MAKING A CLAIM
JOHN 4:43—5:47

REFLECT
on your life

1 Think of a friend or acquaintance who has a crippling physical problem. How did this happen to him/her? How has he/she adjusted to life?

mom /stroke ; she's slowed down, doesn't try to do some of the things she used to do, but has also tried new things (braille typing & painting) Sometimes she feels like giving up

READ
the passage

Read John 4:43—5:47, "The Claims of Christ" chart, and the following notes:

❐ 4:46-49 ❐ 4:50 ❐ 4:51 ❐ 5:10 ❐ 5:17ff ❐ 5:31ff ❐ 5:39,40 ❐ 5:45

2 What are the similarities between the healing of the official's son and the healing of the man by the pool?   — official & man at pool

both had faith to be healed; were healed immediately

3 What are the differences?

Jesus was miles apart from the officials son, but there for the man at the pool. Jesus also told the man at the pool (later) to sin no more - also he was crippled for most of his life.

- direct & indirect

4 What four witnesses of his deity does Jesus appeal to in John 5:33-47?

John the Baptist
God the Father   His works
the Scriptures
Moses

5 If Jesus were not God, why would he make that claim?

liar or lunatic??? power, personal gain

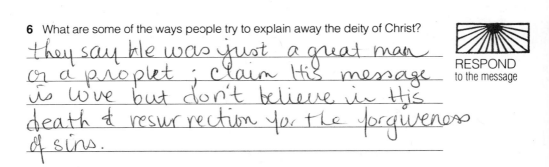

REALIZE
the principle

Some say that Jesus never said he was God, but John quotes Jesus' claim to deity several times. Jesus not only claimed to be God, but he provided miraculous evidence to prove it. Knowing that Jesus is God gives us great confidence when we pray and when we follow his teachings. And having a written record of his life on earth gives real answers to the question "What is God like?" Anyone who wants to know about God has only to look at Jesus.

6 What are some of the ways people try to explain away the deity of Christ?

they say He was just a great man or a prophet; claim His message is love but don't believe in His death & resurrection for the forgiveness of sins.

RESPOND
to the message

7 What would it take to convince people that Jesus is God?

the Holy Spirit, prayer, & the Scriptures. I, on my own, couldn't say anything to convince someone of this.

8 If a person really believes that Jesus is God, what difference should this make in his/her life?

a changed life!

-making Jesus Lord

They should "honor Him and live as Jesus wants them to live". Read the Bible, fellowship w/other believers & constantly be in prayer w/Jesus. Putting away the old & replacing w/the new.

9 What changes might you make to reflect more clearly Christ's divine authority over your life?

more study & prayer. yielding my weaknesses to Him.

RESOLVE
to take action

10 What Bible verse can you memorize or carry with you this week that affirms the deity of Christ in your own mind and that you can use with others?

John 5:22,23 Moreover the Father judges no one, but has entrusted all judgment to the Son, that all may honor the Son just as they honor the Father. He who does not honor the Son does not honor the Father, who sent Him.

MORE
for studying
other themes
in this section

A Explain the statement "a prophet has no honor in his own country"? How does it relate to your attempts to share the gospel?

B What evidence is there in these verses that Jesus came for all people?

C What was the problem with healing the invalid on the Sabbath? When have you let rules or procedures get in the way of helping people? What religious rules do people follow today that are not found in the Bible?

D Why did Jesus heal these people? How do you think Jesus would respond to your request for help?

E When does eternal life begin? How does someone receive eternal life?

F Describe Jesus' relationship with his Father.

REFLECT
on your life

1 What are some right and wrong reasons for going to church?

_____

_____

_____

_____

_____

2 Why do people give up on religion or stop attending church?

_____

_____

_____

READ
the passage

Read John 6:1-71 and the following notes:

❏6:5-7 ❏6:13 ❏6:26 ❏6:28,29 ❏6:41 ❏6:66 ❏6:67,68 ❏6:70

3 At this time in Jesus' ministry, why were people following him?

_____

_____

_____

4 What two sayings of Jesus troubled the Jews?

_____

_____

_____

5 Why did many of Jesus' disciples leave him (6:66)? What was so shocking about Jesus' statement in 6:65?

_____

_____

_____

6 How has God tested your faith?

_____

_____

_____

_____

_____

REALIZE
the principle

7 When has God provided for your needs in a dramatic or miraculous way? How did that affect your faith?

_____

_____

_____

_____

_____

8 What about Jesus do people find difficult to understand or believe today?

_____

_____

_____

_____

Often people followed Jesus for the wrong reasons (e.g., to see a show, to get food, to be healed, etc.). Like the people in John chapter 6, sometimes we also come to him only for what we can get. Jesus asks us to come believing in him, with no strings attached. Many of the people had only defensive responses to Jesus' statements. When God's Word steps on our toes, our best response is humble repentance, not a proud defense. Seeking God with a whole heart, a pure heart, is what pleases him most.

RESPOND
to the message

9 What strings do you find it easy to want to attach to your faith in Christ?

_____

_____

_____

_____

10 In what ways do you follow Christ for what he can do for you, rather than for what you can do for him?

_____

_____

_____

_____

_____

11 How can you begin to follow him more wholeheartedly?

_____

_____

_____

_____

RESOLVE
to take action

12 Complete this statement and make it your prayer: "Lord, I will trust in you and

follow you, even if I don't get _____

_____."

A What evidence for the deity of Jesus does John appeal to in these verses?

B How did Jesus test Philip? Did Philip pass or fail?

C What part did the disciples play in feeding the five thousand? Who else played a part in this miracle? Why do you think Jesus involved other people in this miracle?

D What did the people think about Jesus after he fed the five thousand? What did the disciples think about Jesus after seeing him in action?

E What do you have to offer Jesus that he can use to make a miracle?

F What needs in your life has God met for which you can be thankful?

MORE
for studying
other themes
in this section

REFLECT
on your life

1 What famous people have you met?

Rob Evans - the Donut Man

2 When were you near someone important or famous but you didn't realize it (you learned about it later)?

READ
the passage

Read John 7:1—8:59 and the following notes:

☐7:3-5 ☐7:13 ☐7:19 ☐7:26 ☐7:46-49 ☐7:50-52 ☐7:51 ☐8:32 ☐8:34,35

3 What clues can you find that indicate the following people were religious but far from faith in God: the brothers of Jesus, the crowd in Jerusalem, the Pharisees and other Jewish leaders?

v5 • brothers - did not believe in Him because He wouldn't show himself to the world before His time.

v13 • crowd - wouldn't say anything public about Him, for fear of the Jews

• Pharisees - they were angry because Jesus was putting emphasis on Him & His Father, rather

• Jewish leaders - than the law & they were amazed at His teaching

4 What doubts did the people in the crowds have about Jesus?

They thought He deceived people; thought He was demon-possessed; they knew where He was from, so they didn't think He could be Messiah;

5 What do you think was happening with Nicodemus spiritually?

He was surrending His life to Jesus, acknowledging that He is God. He believed

6 Some people believed in Jesus but were afraid to speak up. What reasons do people give today for not speaking up for Christ?

fear, embarrassment, "inappropriate" timing, lack of knowledge, not wanting to risk the loss of a relationship, avoiding conflict

REALIZE
the principle

7 How are people religious today, yet still far from God?

I hear about people going to church, being involved in their church, boasting of what they do in the church, yet not yielding to what Jesus would have them Be in their personal lives. They talk of church, not of Jesus.
- Focus on works

The Jewish leaders were very religious but not very spiritual. They focused on sin and missed forgiveness, focused on the Sabbath and missed the Lord of the Sabbath, focused on their earthly heritage and missed their heavenly heritage, focused on Jesus' words and missed his message. These people thought they were close to God himself, but they missed him. It is easy for us to do the same. We can be busy about many church activities, even read the Scriptures and pray daily, and still have hearts far from God. We can be close to Jesus and yet miss him completely.

8 What keeps you busy at home? At work? At church?

cleaning house, taking care of kids, helping at school, children's Ministry, 4-H activities, musical, shopping, cooking, errands, phonecalls, transporting Sarah

9 What can absorb so much of your attention that it can cause you to miss Christ?

Everything I do, if I don't put Jesus up front

10 What can you do to be more aware of Christ?

I think I am aware of Christ most of the time, but being aware is not the same as putting Him first — that requires prayer, and an intimate time of fellowship with Him.

11 How can too much religious activity dull you spiritually?

You can get caught up in the busyness of what you're doing — making sure things are getting done, and also pleasing people, rather than taking time to just be with Jesus and remember why you're doing the activity. You lose focus.

12 What can you do to avoid developing a callous, religious mind-set?

Be in the word. Not just go to functions that are "fun" or sociable, but where I am "forced" to get into what God says. Have friends that I can talk about Jesus with, so that He becomes prominent in every aspect of my life.

13 What can you begin doing this week to regain a fresh perspective of Jesus and to renew your mind, heart, and spirit? What will help you get close to God again?

Before I begin any work for Children's Ministry, take time to pray, Make sure He is the leader, and not me. Don't put aside devotionals because I am too busy.
★It AlwAys comes down to prayer★

RESOLVE
to take action

14 What can you do in church this Sunday to see Jesus clearly?

Clear my mind of my week before I go. Be ready to listen to what the Holy Spirit has to say to me. Anticipate!

A What evidence for the deity of Jesus does John appeal to in these verses?

MORE
for studying
other themes
in this section

B Why did the world hate Jesus? How does the world respond to you?

C If you were to ask your neighbors, "Who is Jesus Christ?" what responses would you get? How can you tell them of Christ's true identity?

D Where did Jesus come from? Where did people think he came from? How did this affect how they felt about him?

E What does it mean to be spiritually thirsty? How has the Holy Spirit quenched your spiritual thirst?

F What do you think Jesus wrote in the dirt when he confronted the accusers of the adulterous woman? Why did the older men leave first? How did Jesus respond to the woman and her sin? With whom do you identify in the story?

G In what ways is Jesus the light of your life?

H In what ways has Jesus set you free?

I What was so important about being Abraham's descendants? Who are Abraham's true descendants?

J Why did the Jews want to stone Jesus?

REFLECT
on your life

1 Close your eyes and imagine what it would be like to be totally blind. How would your blindness affect your work and your family life?

_____

_____

_____

2 Now imagine that you were blind and all alone in the world with no means of support. What would you do? How would you live? How would you feel?

_____

_____

_____

READ
the passage

Read John 9:1—10:42 and the following notes:

❒ 9:2,3 ❒ 9:13-17 ❒ 9:25 ❒ 9:28,34 ❒10:1 ❒10:11,12 ❒10:16 ❒10:24

3 What were the doubts of the neighbors?

_____

_____

_____

4 What were the doubts of the Pharisees?

_____

_____

_____

5 How did both these groups respond to their doubts?

_____

_____

_____

_____

6 How did the former blind man describe Jesus?

_____

_____

_____

7 How did the Pharisees respond to his description of Jesus and his questions?

_____

_____

_____

8 How did the former blind man respond when he saw Jesus?

_____

_____

_____

9 How were the Pharisees blind?

_____

_____

_____

REALIZE
the principle

Physical blindness is considered a handicap. It is a world of darkness that many have learned to overcome. Spiritual blindness is a darkness of another kind. It is caused by unbelief. A person can receive spiritual sight just like the blind man received his physical sight—through faith and obedience. He believed the words of Jesus and obeyed him. He went to the Pool of Siloam and washed his eyes. Then hearing that Jesus was the Messiah, he readily believed and worshiped. You and I can receive spiritual sight by hearing the words of Jesus, believing, and willingly responding in obedience. Listen carefully to his words. They are light and sight to the one who hears and obeys.

10 How can we be spiritually blind?

_____

_____

_____

RESPOND
to the message

11 What part does doubt play in spiritual blindness? How has Jesus been a light to you?

_____

_____

_____

_____

12 What unanswered questions or doubts are hindering you from fully trusting the words of Jesus?

_____

_____

_____

_____

13 How has God opened your eyes? What spiritual insights about yourself has God helped you clearly see?

_____

_____

_____

_____

_____

14 What are some areas of spiritual blindness in your life?

_____

_____

_____

_____

15 Pray this week that God would show you one area of your life where you have been blind. This could be in a relationship, at home, at church, at work, or in your devotional life. Pray now that you will be open and responsive to what he has to teach you.

_____

_____

RESOLVE
to take action

16 What will you do this week to begin to resolve your doubts?

_____

_____

_____

_____

A What evidence for the deity of Jesus does John appeal to in these verses?

MORE
for studying
other themes
in this section

B Why was the man born blind? What are some of the reasons God allows suffering and pain in the world? How do you respond to an illness or difficult situation? How could a difficult experience bring glory to God?

C How was the former blind man's faith tested? How has your faith been tested? What can you do to be ready to pass these tests?

D Which name of Jesus means the most to you and why?

E What is the difference between a shepherd and a hired hand? Why is Jesus called "the good shepherd"? How can you have life to the full?

F Who are the "other sheep" in 10:16? Who are the "other sheep" you know who are waiting to hear?

G Why did the people find it so difficult to accept the proof for Jesus' divinity? What would it take to convince people today that Jesus is God?

H Why did the Pharisees want to kill Jesus?

REFLECT
on your life

1 How do people in our society deny mortality, the fact that death is inevitable for everyone?

_____

_____

_____

_____

_____

2 How would you explain death to a six-year-old child?

_____

_____

_____

READ
the passage

Read John 11:1—12:50 and the following notes:

❏ 11:5-7 ❏11:14,15 ❏11:35 ❏12:13 ❏12:16 ❏12:23-25 ❏12:27 ❏12:31

3 What reason did Jesus give for waiting to go to Lazarus?

to bring glory to God – during His time
so that we may believe

4 How did Martha and Mary respond when they saw Jesus?

Martha ran out to meet him but Mary stayed in
the house - they both said if Jesus had been
there then Lazarus would not have died.

✓45

5 Why did Jesus raise Lazarus from the dead? How did people respond to the over death
resurrection?   that Jesus' power ~~could~~ could be show

to reveal God's glory - Many of the Jews put their
faith in him, but some went to the Pharisees to tell
them what Jesus had done. they refused to believe
- rejected him and plotted His murder

5↑

6 How did Jesus face the prospect of his own death?

He didn't go out publicly among the Jews
but stayed in Ephraim (a village near the desert) with
his disciples

7 What can we learn from Martha's conversations with Jesus in verses 21-27
and 39-40?

She believed in Jesus and understood
the resurrection into eternal life,
but did not know or believe that Jesus
would bring Lazarus back to physical life.

REALIZE
the principle

The stark reality is that every person has to die. Many look at death with a sense
of fear: "What lies ahead? . . . Is this life all there is?" Sometimes we react by
holding on to this life, afraid to lose it and afraid to face the next. But the message of Jesus Christ is hope. Though we die, we will be raised again and live
forever with Christ. He is preparing a place for us in heaven and coming back
for us. Instead of fearing death, we can live with confidence. Our confidence is
in his promise and in his demonstration of power over death. Knowing he is
able to raise the dead and that he experienced death himself, we can take comfort in knowing he understands our deepest fears.

8 How do people hold on to life today (12:25)?

being self-centered, striving for security, advantage,
& pleasure - taking control. ~~for~~

9 How can the story of Jesus and Lazarus give us hope?

Jesus proved that he can raise others from the dead - he has the power over life & death, and also to forgive sins

RESPOND
to the message

10 What frightens you most about death and dying?

The pain prior to it and the loss my children (husband) will feel

11 How can this story of Jesus and Lazarus help you prepare for death?

12 What in this life are you holding on to that you need to let go of and lose?

13 Make two lists, one of your fears and one of those things that tend to take priority over Christ in your life. Pray through these lists daily, asking God to remove your fears and giving him anything that stands in the way of total devotion to Christ.

Fears   *Misplaced priorities*

_____   _____

_____   _____

_____   _____

_____   _____

RESOLVE
to take action

A What evidence for the deity of Jesus does John appeal to in these verses?

B Why did Mary and Martha ask Jesus for help? How do you need his help?

C How can troubles be opportunities for honoring Christ?

D What does the story of Jesus and Lazarus teach us about God's timing? When have you tried to hurry God?

E Why did the disciples try to talk Jesus out of going to Jerusalem?

F Why did Jesus cry? What causes his sorrow today?

G Why didn't Lazarus's resurrection convince everyone of Jesus' divinity?

H How did Mary change from chapter 11 to chapter 12? How can you be more like Mary?

I What kind of a person was Judas? Why did Jesus allow him to be a disciple?

J Why did the Jews want to kill Lazarus?

K What were the people expecting when they greeted Jesus at the gates of Jerusalem? What misconceptions do people have about Jesus today?

L Why was Jesus troubled (12:27)?

M What is implied concerning evangelism today in Jesus' statement "But I, when I am lifted up from the earth, will draw all men to myself"?

N What did Jesus mean when he told the disciples to "walk while you have the light" (12:35)? How can we become children of light?

O To whom are you afraid to declare your faith? Of what are you afraid in declaring your faith?

MORE
for studying
other themes
in this section

REFLECT
on your life

1 What is the dirtiest or most distasteful job you ever had to do?

_____

_____

_____

2 Describe a time when you saw a leader, a parent, or someone in authority do a similar kind of work.

_____

_____

_____

READ
the passage

Read John 13:1—14:14, John's Profile, and the following notes:

❑13:1ff ❑13:1-17 ❑13:6,7 ❑13:12 ff ❑13:34 ❑13::34,35 ❑13:35

3 Why was Peter shocked at Jesus' actions?

Because Jesus was his Master - a great
leader, and He was acting like a
slave

_____

_____

4 From what you know about the other disciples, how do you think they felt?

I would imagine they were just as confused as Peter.

5 What reason did Jesus give for washing the disciples' feet?

As an example — They should do for others what Jesus had done for them (be a servant to all) teach them to serve with humility

6 What does it mean to serve others?

Helping, giving, supporting - Doing for them, even when it is inconvenient for us. = helping to make someone else's load easier.

REALIZE
the principle

Jesus not only taught his disciples to be servants, he continually demonstrated servanthood by his actions. In humility, he became a man, served everyone around him, and willingly gave up his life for us. Jesus loves and serves each of us, even though he knows the secret motives of our heart. Jesus told the disciples, and us, to follow his example and serve others. This is what it means to be his *true* disciple.

7 How does Jesus' statement in 13:34, 35 relate to his example of washing the disciples' feet?

Showing sacrificial love - putting others in front of yourself at all times.

8 Describe a true Christian servant you know.

9 When are you like Peter? When are you like Jesus in this story?

RESPOND
to the message

_____

_____

_____

_____

10 Why is it more difficult to serve some people than others?

Because you have a hard time getting along with them, and you feel as if what you do for them will be unappreciated, & they really won't see it's Jesus' love behind the action anyway

11 Whom is it difficult for you to serve?

_____

_____

_____

12 What are some ways you can demonstrate the servant attitude of Jesus in your home? at work? at school? in your church?

Just do things that need to be done without complaining or making excuses .

_____

_____

_____

13 Select one or two specific persons whom you will try to better serve this week.

RESOLVE
to take action

_____

_____

_____

_____

14 What are you going to do to serve them? What is required of you? How could you go above or beyond? What could you do that they would never ask for?

_____

_____

_____

_____

_____

A What evidence for the deity of Jesus does John appeal to in these verses?

B What did Jesus know about his disciples (e.g., Peter, Judas, John)? How did that knowledge affect his actions toward them? How would you treat someone you knew would betray, deny, or desert you? ∧ It didn't.

C How did Jesus respond to Thomas and Philip in chapter 14?

D What hope, from chapter 14, could you share at a funeral?

E What does it mean that Jesus is the way? the truth? the life? How can someone come to the Father through Christ?

F If seeing Jesus is seeing the Father, what have you learned about the characteristics of God the Father?

G What have you asked God for recently in the name of Jesus?

MORE
for studying
other themes
in this section

LESSON 11
A CLOSE RELATIONSHIP WITH CHRIST
JOHN 14:15—17:26

REFLECT
on your life

1 Be very quiet for a moment or two. Listen carefully and write down everything you hear.

clock ticking, refrigerator, train, freeway noise, heater,

2 What's the difference between casual and careful listening? Who listens carefully to you?

casual— not really paying attention to the background noises. careful— is hearing everything.

READ
the passage

Read John 14:15—17:26 and the following notes:

❑14:16 ❑14:17ff ❑15:1ff ❑15:2,3 ❑15:5,6 ❑15:5-8 ❑15:16 ❑15:26

❑16:1-16 ❑17:1ff ❑17:11 ❑17:20

(14:17ff) **3** What does the Holy Spirit do for us?

never will leave us, lives with us & in us, teaches us, reminds us of Jesus' words, convicts us of sin, shows us God's righteousness, announces God's judgement on evil, guides into truth & gives insight into future events, glorifies Christ

4 What does "remaining in Jesus" mean? What are the results of remaining in him?

(15:5,6)

1) believing He is God's son 2) receiving Him as Lord & Savior, 3) doing what God says 4) continuing in faith 5) relating to the community of believers, the church (fellowship)
- Remaining in Him will bear lots of fruit.

5 What kinds of problems and difficulties does Jesus predict for his followers?

persecution, kill them, they will be scattered

6 What resources does Jesus offer us in the face of adversity?

the Holy Spirit, the Word, prayer

REALIZE
the principle

7 What comes to your mind when you hear the word *Counselor*? In what ways is the Holy Spirit our Counselor and Comforter?

counselor - someone to talk to who will objectively help you work through a problem. The H.S. is always there to discuss things with and He helps us in our times of need.

8 How is prayer a resource?

It is our direct line of communication to God.

9 What are the results of praying in Jesus' name?

God answers and gives us what we ask for.

Jesus expressed concern and encouragement to his disciples the night before he was arrested and crucified. His parting words placed strong emphasis on the close relationship offered to everyone who would follow him. Through the work of the Holy Spirit (our Counselor) and our obedience, we can live close to God in a relationship that is compared to the living unity of a grapevine to its branches. Through prayer each one of us is able to approach God directly and tell him the deepest, innermost thoughts of the heart. With great love and understanding, God answers when we pray in the name of Jesus.

RESPOND
to the message

10 What can we do to stay close to Jesus like a branch to the vine?

Be in His will — Pray, stay in the word — fellowship w/other believers

11 What does the Holy Spirit do to nurture our vine-branch relationship with Jesus?

He disciplines us to strengthen our character & faith / cuts back our branches

12 In what ways does God "prune" a fruitful believer? What kind of pruning experiences have you had over the past few months?

God is revealing to me my deeper need of Him, in all areas of my life He has shown me what happens when I separate myself from him. I believe I will grow back more fruitful

13 What new insights has the Holy Spirit revealed to you about God in the past few months? How have those insights affected the way you live?

Constantly convicted of his presence in my life — that I'm the one who strays, not him, and that, even though it is a struggle for me to return, God is waiting w/open arms. When I make the step back, I'm realizing it's not as painful as the guilt & anticipation makes it out to be.

14 What specific answers to prayer have you received in the last three weeks?

— clarity, rather than confusion & depression.
— a peace about the CM. decision

15 What can you do this week to improve your relationship with Christ?

Always the same answer —
pray, Be in the Word

RESOLVE
to take action

16 What one request will you make in prayer this week, expecting God to answer?

MORE
for studying
other themes
in this section

A What evidence for the deity of Jesus does John appeal to in these verses?

B What kind of peace does the world offer us? How does God's peace differ?

C What does it mean to "bear fruit" for Christ? How can we bear fruit for him?

D In what ways has God shown love for you? How can you love others as he has loved you?

E What are the differences between being a servant and a friend of someone? What are the advantages of being God's friend?

F What difference does it make to you that Jesus chose you?

G Why would the world hate followers of Christ? In what ways have you experienced this hatred? How do the world's values differ from yours?

H How is prayer a battleground? How should you improve your prayer life?

I How can Christians have joy?

J How can a person receive eternal life?

K Why does Jesus want his followers to be in the world? How can we change the world for him?

L In what ways can believers be "one"?

1 What public figures have issued denials recently?

REFLECT
on your life

_____

_____

_____

2 As a child, when did you deny the truth, lying to protect yourself?

_____

_____

_____

Read John 18:1—19:42 and the following notes:

❏18:10,11 ❏18:11 ❏18:13 ❏18:22-27 ❏18:31ff ❏18:36,37 ❏19:10 ❏19:18

READ
the passage

❏19:38-42

3 In chapters 18 and 19, what people or groups of people rejected Jesus?

_____

_____

_____

4 To what three different people did Peter deny knowing Jesus? Why did Peter deny Jesus?

_____

_____

_____

5 In what ways do people reject Jesus today?

_____

_____

_____

_____

REALIZE
the principle

6 What are some ways that we deny Jesus today?

_____

_____

_____

_____

_____

7 Who would want to condemn Jesus today?

_____

_____

_____

Everyone around Jesus, including his closest friends, turned his back on him—Judas who betrayed, Peter who denied, the Jewish leaders who condemned, Pilate who accommodated, and the crowd who rejected him. Jesus—the Son of God, the worker of miracles, the proclaimer of truth, the man of compassion—was clearly rejected by all. Jesus had to face the cross utterly alone. Jesus subjected himself to unmerciful punishment to pay the penalty we deserve for our sin. He did not accuse, fight back, or fight for his life. He knew that his purpose was to die for us, in our place. Those who ignore him today reject both his life and his death. Receive his sacrifice and forgiveness. Reject him no more.

8 What kinds of pressure do you feel that make it difficult to identify with Jesus?

_____

_____

_____

_____

_____

RESPOND
to the message

9 In what ways do Christians deny knowing Jesus today? Why do they hesitate to identify with him?

_____

_____

_____

_____

_____

10 How might Christians become more bold, develop more courage, and be more consistent in what they profess?

_____

_____

_____

_____

_____

11 What kind of support from others is needed by someone facing rejection because of his/her faith?

_____

_____

_____

_____

_____

12 What are you going to do this week to build your confidence in being a consistent witness for Christ?

_____

_____

_____

_____

A What evidence for the deity of Jesus does John appeal to in these verses?

B Why did Judas betray Jesus? What misconceptions about Jesus do people have today? How can we tell them the truth about Christ?

C What different kinds of punishment did Jesus endure?

D What were Jesus' responses to Pilate's questions? Why did he answer that way?

E Why did Pilate ask, "What is truth"? How would you answer him? Why did he worry about being Caesar's friend? How did this affect Pilate's actions?

F How is Jesus the King? Where are his subjects and kingdom?

G Who crucified Jesus? Why did Jesus die on the cross? With which person in the story can you identify most (John, Peter, Judas, soldiers, Pilate, Mary, crowd, Nicodemus, Joseph, Barabbas, other)?

H How do we know that Jesus really died on the cross? What difference does that make?

I   In the story, whose lives were changed most by Jesus' death? How has your life been changed by Christ?

MORE
for studying
other themes
in this section

REFLECT
on your life

1 Think back to a time when you said something you knew to be true, but no one believed you? How did you respond to their doubts?

_____

_____

_____

_____

READ
the passage

Read John 20:1—21:25, the profiles of Mary Magdalene and Thomas, and the following notes:

❏ 20:1ff ❏ 20:18 ❏ 20:21 ❏ 20:24-29 ❏ 20:25-28 ❏ 21:15-17 ❏ 21:25

2 How did Mary Magdalene react when she found the stone rolled away?

_____

_____

_____

3 How did the disciples first respond when they found the tomb empty?

_____

_____

_____

4 How did Thomas respond to the words that Jesus was alive? What did it take for him to believe?

_____

_____

_____

5 What evidence for the resurrection does John present?

_____

_____

_____

_____

6 What doubts did you once have about Jesus?

_____

_____

_____

_____

REALIZE
the principle

7 What doubts do you still have about Christianity?

_____

_____

_____

_____

8 For what reason did John write his Gospel (20:31)?

_____

_____

We have all faced doubts about God, the Bible, another person's testimony, and even ourselves. The critical question is, What do we do about our doubts? We can casually ignore God's claims, continually question them, stubbornly resist them, flatly deny them—or look for answers. God tells us to believe and to have faith, but not a blind faith without careful consideration of clear evidence. John

has provided us with ample evidence for a reasonable faith in Jesus Christ. What kind of evidence would you accept? Believe him and find life. "Blessed are those who have not seen and yet have believed" (John 20:29).

RESPOND
to the message

9 What evidence is most convincing to you that Jesus is God's Son and that you need to believe in him?

_____

_____

_____

_____

10 What evidence do you see in other people's lives that Jesus is alive?

_____

_____

_____

11 What kinds of situations or circumstances tend to make your faith falter?

_____

_____

_____

_____

12 What lingering doubts do you have that cause you concern?

_____

_____

_____

_____

13 What would it take for you to resolve those doubts and believe?

_____

_____

_____

_____

14 Rather than denying your doubts, embrace them, try to understand them, and search out the evidence to answer them. With which doubt can you begin? What kind of evidence of God's faithfulness do you need?

_____

_____

_____

_____

_____

RESOLVE
to take action

A What evidence for the deity of Jesus does John appeal to in these verses?

MORE
for studying
other themes
in this section

B How is your life different since you first believed? How can you spread the news about the risen Christ?

C What doubts do your unbelieving friends have? What could you do to help them work through their doubts?

D How does the Bible bring life (20:31)? How can you improve your Bible study?

E What have you learned about Jesus' love from his relationship with Peter? What would your response be if Jesus asked you the questions he asked Peter?

F How did Peter respond to Jesus' questions? What are the "these" that Jesus asked Peter about in 21:15?

G How would you respond to Jesus' question, "Do you love me?"

H Why do we tend to compare our lives with others? How does Jesus' answer to Peter in 21:22 relate to that tendency?

I If the Jews worshiped on Saturday, the Sabbath, what reason would the believers in Christ have for worshiping on Sunday, the first day of the week? How can your worship reflect the truth of the resurrection?